The dream of Great Saigo
大西郷の夢

Masahiro Muramoto

村本正博

南方新社

まえがき

　明治天皇は褒美の名簿としての賞典禄に1869年に署名した。これは明治維新に貢献した人達のための褒美であった。西郷吉之助は藩士としては最高額の2000石を受け取った。

　吉之助は徳川幕府の終焉の日々であった厳しい時代に４年７カ月を罪人として奄美諸島で暮らした。沖永良部島から帰還後、1863年から1873年の間、彼は驚異的な活躍を演じた。彼は薩摩藩士時代と明治政府の参議時代に、公式文書に氏名として隆盛を使った。日常生活では吉之助を使った。混乱を避けるため、この小説の主人公の名は元服以降、彼が使った吉之助である。

　吉之助の母は７人の子を授かった。家族は貧乏であった。しかし、母は快活で楽天的であった。吉之助はどんな時にも決して怒ることはなかった。彼はすべての人に会い、その人の考えを聞いた。彼の雄大な性格はすべての人を魅了した。彼の性格は母の性質が元になっていると考えられた。吉之助の父吉兵衛は、島津斉興、お由良、島津久光に従わなかった。吉兵衛は一貫して島津斉彬を支持していた。

Preface

The Emperor Meiji signed the documents of a premium called Shotenroku in 1869. This was an award government gave as a bonus to a person who contributed a great deal to the Meiji Restoration. Kichinosuke Saigo received 2,000 goku the largest amount.

Kichinosuke had been living in Amami Islands as a criminal for four years and seven months in the hard time of the last days of the Tokugawa shogunate. After the return from Okinoerabu island, he had performed amazing activities from 1863 to 1873.

He signed himself "Takamori" to official documents in his days of the Satsuma clan samurai and a Sangi or top government official of Meiji government. He used Kichinosuke on daily life.

Therefore, to avoid confusion in this book, I use the latter name "Kichinosuke" used since his genpuku, the ceremony of attaining manhood.

The mother of Kichinosuke had seven children. The family was in poverty. However, the mother was cheerful and she was optimistic. Kichinosuke was never in anger. He met and listened to whomever they are. His magnificent character fascinated everybody. His character was considered to take its origin from his mother's nature. The father of Kichinosuke, Kichibei, did not obey Narioki Shimazu. Oyura and Hisamitsu Shimazu. Kichibei had been supporting Nariakira Shimazu consistently.

吉兵衛はお由良騒動で死んだ赤山靭負の血染めの着物を吉之助に見せている。徳川幕府の終焉の時代の薩摩藩を理解するために、お由良騒動の全容を知ってほしいが、本書では紙幅の都合で細かく言及することはない。この件については、他の文献を参照してほしい。
　吉之助の昇進の理由は農業建白書だけではなく、物怖じしない態度と発言力であった。斉彬は言った。
　「西郷吉之助を操縦できるのは俺だけである」

Kichibei showed Kichinosuke bloody clothes of Yukie Akayama who died in Oyura feud. I want you to know the whole picture of Oyura feud to understand the Satsuma clan in the last days of the Tokugawa shogunate.

Though space did not permit me to explain that, I would like you to read other documents about it.

Kichinosuke got a promotion because of not only his memorial of agriculture but also his never timid attitude and powerful voice. Nariakira said.

"I am the only man that can control Kichinosuke Saigo."

大西郷の夢

The dream of Great Saigo

第1章

　西暦1192年に源頼朝は源氏を将軍とする鎌倉幕府を開いた。鎌倉は平治の乱で敗れた父義朝が少年時代を過ごした源氏ゆかりの地である。地方に荘園を持つ藤原氏などの貴族に代わって、全国を支配するため、頼朝は全国に守護と地頭を配置した。守護には武力、地頭には年貢徴収権を与えた。

　頼朝には愛妾との間に子、惟宗忠言がいたが、北条氏との衝突を避けるため、忠言を薩摩の守護に任じた。忠言の子忠久は島津氏を名乗った。すなわち、島津氏は源氏正統の血を引き、秀才頼朝に似て名君が多い。

　島津氏は平氏の影響力の強い蒲生氏、肝属氏、伊東氏などを次々に破り、400年後の戦国末期には薩摩、大隅、日向の三国を領有するに至った。

　1600年、関ヶ原の戦いで西軍に属して、徳川方に敗れたが、島津藩は領土を維持することが出来た。

　1609年に島津藩は奄美諸島と琉球諸島に大軍を派遣した。

　奄美諸島は島津藩に併合され、琉球諸島も島津藩の支配下となった。

　薩摩藩は奄美と琉球の人々に黒糖の納入を命じた。

Chapter 1

In 1192, Yoritomo Minamoto had opened the Kamakura Shogunate that the Shogun was the lord of the Genji clan. Kamakura was the region where Yoritomo's father, the loser of Heiji war, had been growing in boyhood. Kamakura is known for its association with the Genji clan. Yoritomo arranged a protector and the lord of a manor to govern japan instead of a nobleman such as Fujiwara family who had possessed a manor in local land.

He gave the post of protection the army. And he gave the lord of a manor the right of taxation. Yoritomo sent Hirokoto Koremune for the protector of Satsuma. Hirokoto was the son of lover of Yoritomo. The son of Hirokoto, Tadahisa changed the clan name from Koremune to Shimazu.

The Shimazu clan gained many victory by a war. They defeated strong native samurai such as Kamou, Kimotsuki, Itoh. After four hundred years, Shimazu clan occupied three country, Satsuma, Ohsumi and Hyuga,

In 1600, Satsuma clan were defeated by Ieyasu Tokugawa on Sekigahara war. However, Shimazu clan were able to maintain own territory. In 1609, Shimazu clan sent big army to Amami island and Ryukyu island. As the result, all islands were occupied by the Satsuma clan. The Satsuma clan ordered the supply of black sugar to peoples of islands.

西郷吉之助の祖先は肥後の菊池一族であったが、江戸中期に鹿児島の加治屋町に移住し、西郷を名乗った。本家筋ではないが、肥後の名門であるため、城下士の身分を与えられ、代々47石取りの下級武士であった。

　父吉兵衛は子供7人と自分の親2人を養うため、田畑を借り、牛も養っていた。吉之助は幼名を小吉と言い、10歳で早くも5尺4寸もあった。大柄ではあったが、身のこなしが速く、相撲、水泳も得意であった。

　郷中教育の学舎には走って通った。12歳の時、喧嘩の仲裁にはいり、友人の刀で右腕に大怪我をした。一命はとりとめたが、右腕の筋が切れていたため、右腕が不自由となった。このため、剣道の稽古は諦め、学問に精を出すようになった。14歳で元服し、吉之助と名乗り、下加治屋町の二才組にはいった。父は郡方助役という年貢を農民から集める仕事をしていた。吉之助は父の仕事を手伝い、農業に興味を持ち、父の農作業もよく手伝った。17歳になった時、父は吉之助を郡方奉行の迫田利済の家に連れて行った。

　「息子さんは体は大きいが、誠実な目を持っていなさる」。迫田奉行は一目で吉之助を気に入ったようであった。

　父は1年後を目途に引退し、息子吉之助に仕事を継がせたい旨を迫田奉行に伝えた。

The ancestors of Kichinosuke Saigo was the Kikuchi family in Higo. They transferred to Kajiyacho of Kagoshima city in the middle of the Edo period, and changed their family name for Saigo. They were not the head family in the Kikuchi clan, but they were famous family in Higo.

The Satsuma clan gave them the status of the true samurai. The clan gave them the salary of 47 koku.

Kichinosuke's father, Kichibei, rent the fields and kept cattle to support his family, seven children and parents. Kokichi, the childhood name of Kichinosuke, was already 165 cm tall at the age of ten. He was able to run very fast and good at swimming and sumo. He ran to school of the gochu education.

When he was twelve years old, he was seriously injured in the right hand caused his friend's sword due to the arbitration of quarrel. He lost the use of his right hand. He gave up the training of Japanese fencing, Kendo. When other students practice various sports, he read books by oneself. His father, Kichibei, carried out the ceremony of initiation of samurai for Kokichi. At the age of 14, Kokichi changed his name for Kichinosuke. He entered the high class of the Kajiyacho school. Kichibei had engage in taxation work. In spite of the status of Jyokashi, Kichibei engaged in agriculture. Kichibei took Kichinosuke to the home of Toshizumi Sakoda, the magistrate of taxation. "Your son is very big, but he shows sincerity in his eyes."

He said seemed to like Kichinosuke at the first sight. Kichibei proposed to retire from his own post and told the magistrate that he wanted his son to take over it.

迫田奉行は墨、筆、白紙を取り出し、なにやら書き付けていたが、済むと紙を吉兵衛に渡した。吉兵衛は黙って紙を吉之助に渡した。紙には次のように書かれていた。
　辞令
　西郷隆永を郡方助役に任ず
　　　　任命権者　迫田利済
　　　　弘化元年4月1日
　迫田奉行は妻に焼酎の準備をさせ、高座を降り、吉兵衛の側に来て盃を吉兵衛に渡し、焼酎を注いだ。
「私がこの歳まで年貢徴収の仕事ができたのは、ひとえにお奉行様のご指導のたまもので御座います」
「貴殿の多大な成果は私の備忘録に記載されておる。年貢徴収の仕事は本来、郷士の仕事であるが、よくぞ30年もやってくださった。お礼を言うのは私の方だ」
　迫田奉行は若い頃、水戸学を修めた人格者であった。彼は敬天愛人の話をした。
　若い吉之助は水戸学を理解できなかったが、彼はこの人物についてゆくことを決心した。

＊隆永は吉之助の元服時の諱

Magistrate Sakoda took a sheet of paper out of his desk. And he wrote something on this paper. He gave this paper to Kichibei. Kichibei cast a glance on this paper. And he passed it Kichinosuke. The contents were as follows.

Written appointment. We appoint Takanagå Saigo deputy Mayer

        Toshizumi Sakoda, Mayer of south Kagoshima

           April first, the first year of Kouka

Sakoda magistrate ordered the preparation of shochu for his wife, And he came down from own his stage and sat down beside Kichibei. He gave Kichibei a wine cup and poured shochu into it.

"If it were not for your aid, I would never continued my work up to this age. I thank you for your instruction for a long time."

"Your great job has been recorded in my memorandum." "The work of taxation belongs to the one of goshi (coutry samurai) fundamentally." "You had continued this work for thirty years." "I would like to thank you." Sakoda magistrate studied Mito learning in his youth. And he was a person with an admirable character. He talked about the phrase "Revere heaven, love people." Kichinosuke was not old enough to understand the Mito learning. However, Kichinosuke decided to follow Sakoda magistrate.

*note : Takanaga Saigo is Kichinosuke's original name on the family register.

吉之助の近所に住む大久保正助は、3歳年下であったが頭脳明晰で、学問は郷中の中では抜群であった。体は華奢で剣道などは得意ではなかった。下級武士の家柄ではあったが、和漢、洋学の本をたくさん持ち、吉之助に貸してくれた。藩校造士館の講義にも顔をみせ、藩の重役にも一目置かれていた。

　吉之助と正助は郷中教育の中に政治、行政の討論会を取り入れ、この中から松方正義、村田新八などの俊才が輩出した。大久保正助と吉之助は少年時代から政治体制として共和制をすでに議論の対象としていた。

　嘉永4年（1851）、吉之助が24歳の時、42歳の島津斉彬が江戸から薩摩へ藩主として赴任した。その前年、赤山靱負が切腹して、藩内の主導権争いであるお由良騒動は決着していた。斉彬は将軍の人質として江戸に留め置かれたから、鹿児島の地を踏むのは初めてであった。

　自顕流の稽古を見て、斉彬は言った。

　「とても人間業とは思えぬ」

　最初に打ち込む時、猿のような奇声を発するからである。実父斉興とその愛妾お由良に疎遠にされながらも、すんなり藩主に収まったのは筆頭老中阿部正弘の支持と英才ぶりが内外に知られていたからであった。

　吉之助はお由良騒動の経緯を観察し、斉彬赴任の前年には斉彬派になっていた。

＊大久保正助は、後の大久保利通

Shosuke Okubo* has been living in neighborhood. He was three years junior to Kichinosuke. He has been having clear brain and he was good at every learning in learning school.

Although he was a true samurai of low status, he has been already reading many books of japan and China. He lent these books to Kichinosuke. He also attended the lecture of clan school Zoshikan. The executive samurais of the Satsuma clan has been remarking about Shosuke's ability. Kichinosuke and Shosuke became to the leader of high school class. Two young samurais contained political science and administration in gochu education.

In February 1851, Nariakira Shimazu, 42 years old, promoted to the lord of the Satsuma clan from Edo when Kichinosuke was 24 years old. He came to Kagoshima for the first time because he had to stay in Edo as a hostage so far.

In 1850, Oyura feud was solved by the harakiri of Yukie Akayama.

Seeing the trainning of Jigenryu fencing, he said. "Their prowess cannot be the work of man."

On the first attack, they made strange cries like monkeys. Although Nariakira was hated by Narioki and Oyura, he was promoted to the lord of the clan smoothly. That was because of the support of Masahiro Abe, principal retainer of the shogunate, and the widespread recognition of high ability of Nariakira. One year before Nariakira's promotion, Kichinosuke belonged to the Nariakira group, observing the circumstances behind Oyura feud.

* note : Toshimichi Okubo used Shosuke for his another name in daily life.

吉之助は25歳の時、親戚の世話で、伊集院須賀と結婚した。ところが、その年の9月に父吉兵衛、11月に母マサが相次いで死去した。家庭の働き手が急にいなくなり、妻須賀の苦労は並大抵ではなかった。結婚後3年で貧窮を見るに見かねた実家の伊集院家が須賀を強引に引き取ってしまった。吉之助はやむなく離婚を受け入れた。その後吉之助は年貢徴収、農作業、家事労働で目のまわるような忙しさであった。

　嘉永5年（1852）、吉之助は家督相続を藩から許された。

　吉之助は公務のない時間は自ら牛を引いて、農作業に従事した。薩摩はシラスと呼ばれる火山灰混じりの痩せた土壌のため、米、麦、野菜などが他藩にくらべ、質と量が劣った。彼は10年間の経験をもとに、農業技術の観点から建白書を書き、藩主斉彬公に提出した。

　斉彬公はこの建白書に注目し、そのころ反射炉を建設中であった集成館に吉之助を呼びつけた。

　庭に正座した吉之助を見て、斉彬公はその風貌に驚いた。

　大きな目玉は鳶色に澄み切り、意志の強そうな太い眉毛、身長は6尺はあろうか。このような威風堂々とした男を斉彬公は見たことがなかった。藩主を前にして臆するところはなかった。

Kichinosuke married Suga Ijyuin by a relative when he was 25 years old. But in September, father Kichibei and in November, mother Asa died successively in this year. With the sudden loss of workers, Suga had hard days of full of troubles. Three years after their marriage, the father of Suga could not stand to see her in poverty such a state of fatigue. He brought his daughter back home compulsorily. Kichinosuke accepted the divorce unwillingly. After that, Kichinosuke was very busy with official work and house keeping. In 1852, the Satsuma clan permitted Kichinosuke to succeed to his house.

Kichinosuke was engaged in agricultural work while he had no official work. The Satsuma territory had three volcano such as Sakurajima, Kaimondake and Kirishima. There was a lot of volcanic soil in the most area. The quality and quantity of rice was inferior to an other clan. Kichinosuke submitted written memorials on agriculture technique to the lord of the clan writing based on his 10 year experience.

The lord of the clan, Nariakira, was interested in this report and had Kichinosuke come to Syuseikan factory where a reverberating furnace was under construction at that time. Nariakira surprised at the appearance of Kichinosuke when he saw him sitting in the garden. His big reddish brown eyes were clear. He had thick eyebrows that showed a strong will. Also, he was such a tall man that seemed to reach a height of six feet.

Nariakira had never seen such a stately man such as Kichinosuke. Kichinosuke was never timid in front of the lord of the clan.

「貴殿の建白書は読ませてもらった。確かに問題点は指摘している。しかし、将来の展望についてはなにも書かれていない。考察は初期段階で終わっている」

斉彬公の評価は厳しいものだった。しかし、この日斉彬公は意外な思想を披露してくれた。

「昨年のペルリ来航以来、外国船打ち払いの思想、いわゆる攘夷の思想が日本に蔓延しつつある。しかし、これは米国、ヨーロッパの軍事力を知らぬ者の戯言である。日本は清国の二の舞いにならぬよう海軍力をもたねばならぬ。外国に頼らず自前で大砲や銃を作り、西洋型の軍事演習を実行するのじゃ」

「米国、ヨーロッパの開港要求にはどう対処するのですか」。吉之助は鋭く斬り込んだ。

「開港と条約締結をすべての国に約束するのじゃ。ただ、上陸と占領を許さぬ事が肝要じゃ」

斉彬公の大胆な思想に吉之助は仰天した。集成館には肥前藩主、鍋島直正公が来ていた。斉彬公は直正公に吉之助を紹介した。その後、言った。

「我々は今反射炉を建設している。銑鉄を作るには反射炉を2000度以上の高温にする必要がある。その後、銑鉄は大砲の砲身を作るため、鋳型の中に流し込まれる」

"I had already read your written memorial. Your petition pointed out some questions. However, you had never written about a future prospect. The consideration ended on the initial stage." The evaluation on the petition of Nariakira were very hard. However, Nariakira introduced unexpected thought in this day.

"There has been expanding thought of the exclusion of foreigners since the visit of Perry last year. This is the delusion of foolish men who are unable to understand the army power of foreign countries such as Europe and America. We must have the strong navy power to avoid making the same mistake of Shin kingdom of China. We must make a big gun and a short gun by ourselves without the help of foreign country. We must hold maneuvers exercises in western style."

"How cope with the request of foreign country on the opening of trade port." Kichinosuke keenly asked about the difficult question.

"It is important for Japan to promise the opening of the port and the union of a treaty between all the country. But, we never permit the landing and the occupation of our country area."

Kichinosuke surprised at a bold idea of Nariakira. Naomasa Nabeshima, the lord of the Hizen clan, had come to the factory. Nariakira introduced Kichinosuke to Naomasa. "We have been constructing reverberating furnace. Two thousand degrees of high temperature in the furnace need to make pig iron. Then the pig iron is poured into a mold to make the main body of a big gun."

「我々は砲身の内側に青銅を塗る。青銅は薩摩には少ない」

斉彬は、肥前藩の概要を説明した。

「肥前佐賀には鋳物職人が多い。また、大砲を作るのに良い条件を持っている」。吉之助は直正公が斉彬の技術を盗みに来たのを理解した。

直正公は斉彬から反射炉の建設技術を学んでいた。そして斉彬は直正公から青銅の塗布技術を学んでいた。

安政元年（1854）、建白書が認められた。彼の建白書の一部は、藩の農業技術に採用された。吉之助は中御小姓、江戸勤務を命ぜられた。近思録を輪読する会の同志、大久保正助、税所篤、吉井友実、伊地知正治、有村俊斎らも吉之助の出世に大喜びであった。この頃、下級武士が江戸の薩摩藩邸に勤務する可能性はなかった。

「兄じゃ西郷家はおいとうっかたと信吾が守いもんで心配しやんな。兄さんは、我々兄弟の誇りじゃ」と次弟吉二郎が言ってくれた。

藩主斉彬は天保山で軍事演習をしながら、京都では篤姫を近衛家に送り込み、将軍家定との結婚準備を進めていた。篤姫は将軍家定が病弱であることを知らされてはいなかった。吉之助の最初の仕事は家定と篤姫の公式面会であった。

"We must coat bronze inside a big gun. Bronze is in short supply in Satsuma." Nariakira explained the summary of the Hizen clan.

"The Hizen clan has many casting craftsman, Also, they have good condition for making big gun." Kichinosuke understood that Naomasa has been stealing the technique of Nariakira.

Naomasa learned about the technique of the construction of the furnace from Nariakira and Nariakira learned about to coat Bronze from Naomasa.

In 1854, the written memorial of Kichinosuke was adopted. The part of his plan were contained into agricultural technique. Kichinosuke became the secretary of Neriakira and he was ordered the transfer to Edo. The companion of gochu education such as Okubo, Yosii, Ijichi pleased with the promotion of Kichinosuke. There is no possibility that the samurais of low status work on the office of the Satsuma clan of Edo.

"Elder brother, do not mind about your family." "My wife will take care of your younger sister." "You are the pride of our family." Kichijiro, his younger brother, said to Kichinosuke. Nariakira transferred Atsuhime from Kyoto to Edo based on the recommendation of Masahiro Abe. Atsuhime was never informed the situation that the Shogun Iesada was struggled with dementia. The first work of Kichinosuke was the first formal meeting of Iesada and Atsuhime.

第2章

　斉彬、篤姫、吉之助は江戸城の大広間の中央に座っていた。将軍家定は高座の上に若い二人の武士と共に座っていた。老中首座阿部正弘がすべての出席者に言った。
　「薩摩藩主、斉彬公が篤姫様を紹介します」
　「篤姫様は輿入れ後、敬子と名を変えられます。彼女は公家近衛家で作法を学んできました。彼女は妻として心を込めて上様のお世話をするに違いありません」。斉彬公は説明した。
　将軍家定公は子供の頃からひ弱な体であった。老中阿部正弘は斉彬公に言った。
　「わが殿は、午前中ずっと悪い風邪で床についておられました」
　家定公は病人のように見えた。
　「私は指宿の海岸で育ちました。上様のお世話をさせていただきます」。篤姫は言った。
　将軍家定公は極めて病弱で人と話すことを極端に嫌った。しかし、将軍の青白い顔には薄い赤みがさしていた。彼は篤姫が自分の妻であると理解することは出来た。
　しばらくして、家定公は体を重そうにして隣の部屋に移った。斉彬公は自分の困難な仕事のために藩邸へ帰った。

Chapter 2

Nariakira, Atsuhime and Kichinosuke were sitting on the center of straw matting room of Edo Castle. Shogun Iesada sit down with two young samurai on the stage. Masahiro Abe, top principal retainer said to all the attendants. "The lord of the Satsuma clan, Nariakira shall introduce Atsuhime."
"Atsuhime will change her name for Sumiko after the marriage." "She has been learning the manner of the Court in Konoe family." "She is sure to take care of the Shogun sincerely as his wife."
Shogun Iesada had been weak since childhood. Masahiro Abe, principal retainer said to Nariakira. "Our lord has been in bed with a bad cold all this morning." Iesada seemed to be a sick man. "I have grown on the beach of Ibusuki." "I will take care of my lord."
Shogun Iesada could not speak due to dementia disease. However, a slight flush soon came to Shogun's pale cheeks. He understand that Atsuhime was his own wife. In a few minute, Iesada moved to the next large room as if his own body was so heavy. Nariakira came back to the clan mansion for his difficult work.

江戸の薩摩藩邸に着いた日に篤姫は女中の話を耳にした。

「公方様はアメリカのハリス様に挨拶もできなかったそうよ」「江戸城に通訳はいるのにね」

　覚悟はしていたものの篤姫の衝撃は大きかった。

　1カ月後、盛大な披露宴が江戸城内で挙行された。篤姫は花嫁の席に座り、堂々と大名達の挨拶を受けた。その姿は人々の涙を誘った。

　水戸藩は、一橋家に入った徳川斉昭の実子慶喜の将軍就任をめざしていた。

　斉彬は吉之助に水戸藩、越前藩への工作を命じた。

　安政元年（1854）4月、吉之助は藤田東湖を訪問した。藤田は斉昭を水戸藩主に押し上げたことで功績があり、藩の天保の改革でも活躍した。

　吉之助と同じ江戸詰めの樺山三円は、桜の満開の頃、小石川の水戸藩邸を訪問した。

　東湖は視野が広く、吉之助と三円は深い感銘を受けた。人好きのする吉之助は、水戸に多くの友人が自然に出来た。

　しかし、水戸も一枚岩ではなく、南紀派と言われる井伊の切り崩しが進んでいることがわかった。安政2年10月の地震で東湖は亡くなり、吉之助は悲しみに暮れた。

Atsuhime listened maid servant were speaking on the day of the arrival at Edo. "The Shogun could not exchange a greeting with Mr. Harris of the minister of the United States." "The Shogunate have the interpreter in Edo Castle." The shock of Atsuhime was very strong, even if she was ready. After a month, the wedding reception were held on a grand scale in Edo Castle. Atsuhime sat down on the seat of the bride and stately received greeting of all the daimyo. Her attitude moved people to tears. The Mito clan aimed the promotion Yoshinobu Tokugawa, the son of Nariaki, to the shogun who had been adopted as a son of the Hitotsubashi clan.

Nariakira ordered Kichinosuke the manipulating of the Mito clan and the Echizen clan,

In April, 1854, Kichinosuke visited Toko Fujita of the Mito clan. Toko Fujita had the achievement on the promotion Nariaki to the lord of the Mito clan. Also, he was active on the Tenpo reform of the Mito clan. Kichinosuke and San-en Kabayama, colleague of the clan, visited the clan mansion of the Mito clan in Koishikawa of Edo when cherry blossoms were full bloom everywhere. Tohko had a wide view, which impressed Kichinosuke and San-en deeply. Thanks to Toko's broad relation ship and Kichinosuke's friendly character, Kichinosuke naturally made many friends in Mito. But, the Mito clan, was not simple one group. Naosuke Ii of south Kishu group had been splitting the Mito clan. In 1858, Toko died in the big earthquake. Kichinosuke were in deep sorrow.

東湖と会った翌月、吉之助は江戸の越前藩邸に橋本左内を訪ねた。

左内は福井藩士として藩医の家に生まれた。安政2年（1855）に明道館が設立されると、学監心得に任ぜられた。彼は藩の教育改革を実行して実績をあげた。彼は松平春嶽のもとで次期将軍に一橋慶喜を推薦していた。

橋本左内は吉之助に挙国一致の政治体制を説いた。

「世界は将来五大陸が一つになり、盟約を選び、世界各地の戦乱は収まるであろう」

「日本が独立するには蒙古、満州、朝鮮を併合し、アメリカ大陸またはインドに属領を得る必要がある」

「ロシアと同盟を結んで富国強兵の国にしなければならない」

「次期将軍をすみやかに決め、諸藩の有能な人物を中心にすえ、身分にかかわらず国政に人材を登用することが肝要である」

吉之助はその大胆な発想に驚嘆した。左内は啓発録を著し、自らを律した。吉之助にそのいくつかを伝えた。

「幼い心を捨てなければならない」

「目標に達するまでの道筋を多くしないことが肝要である」

「目標を達成するまでどこまでも続けねばならない」

「男子は国家が安定しているか、危機に直面しているかを常に考えねばならない」

In the next month after the meeting with Toko, Kichinosuke visited Sanai Hashimoto in Echizen clan mansion. Sanai was born in the family of the clan doctor as a samurai of the Fukui clan. When the Meidokan was established in 1855, he was appointed as school supervisor. He carried out educational reform. And he gained the good result. He had been recommending Yoshinobu Hitotsubashi as next Shogun, He explained Kichinosuke the political system of the method of the union of whole nation.

"In the world. The five continents will become united and select the leader of the confederation, then wars around the world will stop in the future." "To become an independent nation, we need to occupy Mongolia, Manchuria, Korea."

"And, we need to gain some territory in the American continent and India."

"We must make the nation wealthy and the military strong allied with Russia."

"It is important for us to decide the next Shogun as soon as possible, and to put competent persons of clans in the center post of the Shogunate." "Also, it is important to select and involve capable persons in national politics, regardless of their status."

Kichinosuke surprised at his brave idea. He controlled himself by writing the self-development book. He told Kichinosuke some platform.

"We must abandon an infant mind." "Only one roads lead to our goal."

"You must continue the effort until the achievement of your objective." "A man must always know if the nation is stable or in a crisis."

第3章

　アメリカのペリー来航以来、幕府内で開国派の井伊直弼と攘夷派の老中筆頭阿部正弘の対立は激しくなった。

　阿部は水戸藩の徳川斉昭を海防顧問として幕政に参加させた。一方、斉昭は攘夷を主張した。安政4年（1857）に、将軍家定は寝たきりになった。直弼は紀州の家茂を将軍に推薦した。直弼は下田奉行や京都守護職を歴任し、公家との人脈が多かった。安政5年（1858）に井伊は大老に就任した。

　外人嫌い、攘夷派の孝明天皇は8月8日に水戸藩に秘密の勅令を送った。その内容は、外国人退去を水戸藩の手で実行せよというものだった。梅田雲浜が計画したと言われている。

　江戸時代に朝廷が藩に直接命令したことはなかったので、井伊は激怒した。井伊は許可なしの江戸城入りなどの理由をつけて、徳川斉昭、松平春嶽に蟄居、謹慎、梅田雲浜、橋本左内らを死罪とした。徳川慶喜も登城禁止の処分を受けた。多くの攘夷武士が逮捕され、死罪、流刑となった。薩摩の島津斉彬は開国論者でかつ領国勤務であったため、刑を受けなかった。

　井伊は朝廷の許可を得ぬまま、日米修好通商条約に調印した。

Chapter 3

Since visit to Japan of Perry of the United States, Naosuke Ii and Masahiro Abe conflicted hardly. Ii claimed the opening country and Abe claimed the exclusion of foreigners. On the other hand, Abe made Nariaki Tokugawa participate in the politics of the Shogunate as the consultant of coast defense. Nariaki contended over the exclusion of foreigners in 1857. Shogun Iesada came to be confined in his bed. Naosuke recommended Iemochi as the next Shogun.

Naosuke Ii successively hold the post of Kyoto protection and Shimoda Magistrate. He had a lot of contact with many court nobles. In 1858, Naosuke Ii gained the post of the chief minister of the Shogunate. Emperor Komei a xenophobe send a secret order to the Mito clan in August 8. The content of the order was that the Mito clan should perform the exclusion of foreigners. It is said that Unpin Umeda had made the plan. Because the Court never give the order for a clan in Edo period. Naosuke Ii got very angry. Naosuke Ii imposed the penalty of his confinement on Nariaki and Shungaku for entering Edo Castle without permission and Ii gave the death penalty for Unpin Umeda and Sanai Hashimoto. Yoshinobu Tokugawa was forbidden from going to Edo Castle.

Many Jyoi samurais were arrested and given death penalty or sent to island. Nariakira had no penalty due to his thought of opening country and the work on his territory. Naosuke Ii signed Treaty of Amity and Commerce between Japan and America without the permission of the Court.

斉彬は将軍継嗣問題で井伊に敗れた。斉彬は彦根藩との戦争を計画した。連日、海岸の天保山で軍事演習をしていた。
　安政5年（1858）7月、斉彬は帰城後、病に倒れ1週間後の7月16日に死去した。悲報は京都にいる吉之助にもすぐもたらされた。
　吉之助は2日間泣き続けた。そして、殉死を決意した。
「貴方が死んで斉彬公が喜ぶでしょうか。貴方は斉彬公の遺志を継がねばなりません」
　吉之助は月照の説得で死を思い止まった。
　京都には吉之助と月照の人相書きが出回り、身に危険が迫っていた。月照の元勤務寺、清水寺に身を隠していたが、ここも危険となった。
　平野国臣が知らせてくれた。
「大阪経由で船に乗り、まず下関へ行き、薩摩に帰りましょう」
　吉之助は刀を国臣に預け、力士の格好をした。大阪港に着くと有村雄介が待っていた。
「水戸では武士が脱藩して、井伊の命を狙っている。弟の次左衛門も仲間に加わっている。井伊の思うがままにはさせぬ」
　鹿児島では斉彬の遺言により、久光の子、忠義が藩主となっていた。

Nariakira was defeated by Naosuke Ii on the problem of the successor of the Shogun. Nariakira planed the war against to the Hikone clan. Satsuma soldiers trained on the beech of Tenpozan every day. In July 1858, he was downed by a disease.

A week later on July 16, he died. The sad news were reported to Kichinosuke who was staying in Kyoto. Kichinosuke had sobbed for two days. And he decided to immolate himself on the death of his lord.

"The lord, Nariakira, shall be never pleased even if you died." "You must carry out his wishes of the lord of the clan, Nariakira."

Kichinosuke stopped killing himself after the persuasion of Gessho. A lot of description of Gessho and Kichinosuke were stuck on a fence in Kyoto.

The danger had been approaching to the both men. They were hidden in Kiyomizudera Temple, the old work place of Gessho. But there became the dangerous place. Kuniomi Hirano informed Kichinosuke of the danger. "We shall go to Osaka and then back to Satsuma by way of Shimonoseki by ship." Hirano said to Kichinosuke. Kichinosuke left own swords to Hirano. Kichinosuke pretended to Sumo wrestler. Yusuke Arimura was waiting on Osaka port. "Many samurais left the Mito clan." "They are trying to kill Naosuke Ii." "My younger brother, Jizaemon, also joined to the masterless samurais of Mito. We will never allow Ii to do as he like so." In Kagoshima, Tadayoshi Shimazu promoted to the Lord of the clan in accordance with Nariakira's will.

薩摩藩では久光が実権を握っていた。彼は幕府の追及を恐れ西郷は死亡したと報告した。4人は藩校造士館に隠れた。心配した大久保正助が来た。彼は藩主忠義公の命令書を読み上げた。

「西郷吉之助を東目送りとする」

　東目は日向を指していた。護送して日向にはいったらすぐ斬り殺すのである。大久保は鹿児島港まで見送った。4人と監視役人2人が同乗した。船は国分港をめざして出発した。昼過ぎに船は吉野村の沖を走っていた。湾内なので波は静かである。

　月照は静かに酒を飲んでいた。彼は孝明帝の教育係をして、勤王の志士にとって尊敬の的であった。月照は紙と筆を取り出し、何やら書き付けた。

　　大君のためには何か惜しからむ
　　　　薩摩の瀬戸に身は沈むとも

　月照は立ち上がると、いきなり身をひるがえして海に飛び込んだ。これを見た吉之助も海に飛び込んだ。

「二人を助けろ。日向に着いたら俺たちがどうにかする」

　国臣が叫んだ。

「縄と網が要る。漁師を20人くらい集めろ」

　4時間後、吉之助と月照は見つかり引き上げられた。月照は死んだが吉之助は息を吹き返した。

Hisamitsu Shimazu had taken the political power in the Satsuma clan. He was afraid of the power of the Shogunate. And he reported that Kichinosuke Saigo had already died. Gessho and three samurais hid in Zoshikan of clan school. Shosuke Okubo visited clan school anxiously. He read the order document of Tadayoshi, the lord of the Satsuma clan. "Kichinosuke Saigo should be sent to an eastern country."

The eastern country meant Hyuga. When a criminal was sent to Hyuga, he was supposed to be killed instantly. Okubo saw four person off at Kagoshima port. Four men and two officers took on the same ship.

The ship started to Kokubu harbor port. The ship was running off shore of Yoshino village in the afternoon. The sea was calm due to Kinko bay. Priest Gessho had been drinking sake calmly. He had engaged in educational officer of Emperor Komei. And he had been respected by Jyoi samurais. He took a sheet of paper and a writing brush out of chest. He wrote something on the paper.

"I will give everything to the Emperor, even if my body is sunken in the sea of Satsuma."

As soon as he stood up on the ship, he suddenly dived into the sea. Loking at this, Kichinosuke also dived into the sea. "Help those two fellows, I will manage to help them when we arrive at Hyuga." Kuniomi cried.

"We need some ropes and nets." "Gather about 20 of fisherman." Four hours later, Kichinosuke and Gessho were found and pulled up to the coast, Gessho had already died but Kichinosuke began to breathe.

第4章

　月照は死んだが、吉之助は生き残った。この事実は吉之助に精神的重圧としてのしかかった。また、4時間も海底に沈んでいた体へのダメージは強く、吉之助は吉二郎宅に寝かされ、回復に3週間かかった。藩は墓を2カ所作り、調査に来た幕府役人に見せた。吉之助は月照を失った衝撃で元気がなく、3週間ほとんど言葉を発しなかった。11月末まで同志の税所篤が吉之助の看病にあたった。

　藩は吉之助と月照の死を幕府に報告し、吉之助の奄美大島配流を決めた。12月、菊池源吾と変名し、山川港に移動した。安政6年（1859）1月4日、大久保正助、伊地知正治、堀次郎らの見送りを受けて山川港を出港した。1月12日に奄美大島龍郷村阿丹崎に着いた。

　吉之助の住居は笠利湾に面していた。茅葺きの小さな家であった。目玉の大きい巨人が突然住み着いたので、近所の子供がおそるおそる覗きに現れた。吉之助が体を起こすと、歓声をあげて逃げ去った。大久保正助、税所篤、吉井友実らから手紙、漬け物、本などが届いた。吉之助も必ず返書を書いた。

「菊池殿は鹿児島の郷中教育の指導者だったと聞いておる」

Chapter 4

Although Gessho had died, Kichinosuke left alone. This reality put pressure on him. As he had been under the sea water for four hours, his body considerably got damaged. He lay down in Kichijiro's home, his younger brother. It took him three weeks to recover. The Satsuma clan made two graves. They were shown to the officer of the Shogunate.

Kichinosuke was in low spirits by because of the death of Gessho and was not able to speak for almost three weeks. Atsushi Saisho, Kichinosuke's comrade, took care of Kichinosuke until the end of November. The lord of the clan, Tadayoshi, reported the death of Kichinosuke and Gessho. He decided the exile of Kichinosuke to Amami-oshima. In December, he changed his name for Gengo Kikuchi and moved to Yamagawa. On January 4, 1859, He departed from Yamagawa sent off of Okubo, Ijichi and Hori. On January 12, he arrived at Anizaki, Tatsugo village. The residence of Kichinosuke faced to Kasari bay. The home was a small one covered with straw-thatch. The news of a giant man with big eyes made children in the neighborhood come to timidly see Kichinosuke. When he stand up his body, they escaped with a cheer. Letters, pickles, and books were sent by Okubo, Saisho, and Yoshii. Kichinosuke wrote the letter in return for a gift.

"I had heard you had been the instructor of the gochu education in Kagoshima."

島に赴任している役人の木場伝内が言った。

「私が読み書き、計算などを教えましょう」

伝内は教室、紙、筆、机などを準備してくれた。生徒は12名が集まった。

吉之助は自ら字を書き、読んでみせた。海岸から貝をたくさん拾ってきて、足し算、引き算、かけ算、わり算を教えた。

吉之助の温かい人柄は子供達にすぐ伝わり、懐いてくれた。親がよく寺子屋の様子を見にきた。

龍郷村の南に名瀬村があり、サトウキビの製糖工場があった。搾りの作業は人力でやる。黒砂糖の量は、持ち込まれたサトウキビの量によるので、不正があればすぐわかり大騒ぎになる。泥棒として捕まるのは必ず善良でおとなしい農民である。

吉之助は監督にあたる役人が犯人であることをつきとめ、収監されていた農民を解放してやったことが何度もあった。

伝内は龍家の娘、於戸間金を吉之助に紹介した。吉之助は寺子屋の手伝いを於戸間金にしてもらった。

吉之助は僧月照の一生を彼女に話した。

「先生の気持ちはわかりますが、元気を出して下さい。

私がお側にいますから」。於戸間金は励ましてくれた。

Dennai Koba, island officer, said.

"I will teach children reading, writing and calculation." Kichinosuke answered to Dennai. Dennai prepared the classroom, paper, writing brush, and desks. Twelve students gathered. Kichinosuke showed them how to read and how to write by himself. He gathered shells on the beach and taught addition, subtraction, multiplication and division using the shell. The warm character of Kichinosuke attracted children and they came to like Kichinosuke. Their parents visited the classroom many times. Nase village neighboring Tatsugo village had productive factory of black sugar. The work of squeezing of sugar cane were performed by man power. The output of sugar had correlation with the quantity of sugar, so everyone was able to notice any dishonesty. And that caused a big loss every time. Good and quiet farmers were arrested as robbers every time. Kichinosuke found out that island officers observing farmers were true robbers and made a farmer to be free many times.

Dennai introduced Otomakane in Ryu family to Kichincsuke. He had Otomakane help with the work of learning school. Kichinosuke told about the death of Gessho to Otomakane. "I understand how you feel, but please cheer yourself up. I will be with you any time if you want."

Otomakane encouraged Kichinosuke.

於戸間金は突然吉之助の家を訪問した。奄美の夕刻は風があるので意外と涼しい。吉之助は海岸に案内した。琉球松が点在し、草がわずかに生えている。水がないので、毒蛇ハブの出る心配はない。
　二人は並んで腰を下ろし、海を見ていた。わずかに波の音が聞こえる。
「役人は伝内様のような立派な人ばかりだと良いのですが。菊池様の勇気には驚きました」
「わしの流刑は当然と思うておる。しかし、橋本左内の死罪はひどすぎる。左内は日本の宝であった。夕べは焼酎を飲みながら、涙が出てのう」
　いつのまにか、於戸間金は吉之助の腕の中にいた。吉之助は於戸間金を寝かせて唇を吸った。
　1カ月後、吉之助は伝内の媒酌で結婚した。吉之助は於戸間金に愛加那という名を与えた。翌年、愛加那は菊次郎を産んだ。江戸では桜田門外で井伊大老が水戸浪士に殺害された。幕府の開国路線が後退し、攘夷の風が吹き始めていた。鹿児島では三弟の竜庵が茶坊主から還俗して信吾と名乗った。
　久光公は公武合体として朝廷と将軍家の婚姻を模索していたが、京都には手づるがなかった。
　大久保は京都に人脈を持つ吉之助の召還を主張した。

One day Otomakane visited Kichinosuke suddenly. It was unexpectedly in the evening in Amami due to sea wind. Kichinosuke introduced Otomakane around the beach. Ryukyu pine were scattered and little grass was growing. Sandy soil had little water. A poisonous snakes shall never appear.

The couple sat down side by side seeing the sea. They were able to hear the small sound of the waves.

"We want to have good island officer such as Mr. Dennai. I surprised at the courage of you, Mr. Kikuchi."

"I think my exile is natural. However, it was hard treatment for Sanai Hashimoto to had been received the death penalty. Sanai was the treasure of Japan. I was shedding tears while drinking Sake last night."

Otomakane was in the arm of Kichinosuke unnoticed. Kichinosuke laid down her on the grass and he gave her a kiss. A month later, Kichinosuke married Otomakane through the good offices of Dennai. Kichinosuke gave Otomakane the name of Aikana. Next year, Aikana had Kikujiro. In Edo, Naosuke Ii was killed by masterless samurais of the Mito clan on the outside of Sakurada gate. The policy of opening the country of the Shogunate weakened. The storms of the Jyoi began to sweep. In Kagoshima, the third younger brother Ryoan, changed his name for Shingo Saigo. He returned to secular life from a tea server to a samurai. The father of the clan, Hisamitsu had been trying to find out the way of the marriage of Shogun and his younger sister of Emperor Komei. But, he had no connection in Kyoto. Okubo affirmed about the return of Kichinosuke who had a lot of connection in Kyoto. (Jyoi =exclusion of foreigners).

文久元年（1861）11月、島津忠義公は龍郷の見聞役木場伝内に吉之助の召喚状を送った。この年愛加那は二番目の子を身ごもっていた。

　流人の島妻は鹿児島に連れて帰れないので、愛加那は驚かなかった。

　文久２年（1862）１月14日、吉之助は阿丹崎にいた。愛加那は菊次郎の手を引き連れてきた。

「私はお前と暮らして元気を取り戻した。お前の援助を決して忘れない」

「あなたは大きな野心を持っています。成功を信じています」

　菊次郎は父の大きな体をみていた。多くの島民が吉之助を見送った。

　吉之助は２月12日に鹿児島に着いた。吉之助は翌日、鶴丸城二の丸に久光公を訪問した。藩主の忠義公も来ていた。

　久光公は京都行きの準備をしていた。

「何のための上京でごわすか」。吉之助は久光公に聞いた。

「和宮様の輿入れが実現したので、今度は幕府幹部の入れ替えじゃ」

「恐れながら申し上げます」

「殿は鹿児島では絶大な権力をお持ちですが、京都、江戸では無位、無冠です。上京はおやめになったが良いと存じます」

In November 1861, Tadayoshi Shimazu sent the summons document on Kichinosuke to Dennai Koba, the inspector of Tatsugo village. Aikana was going to have the second child. Aikana was never surprised to hear the news because island wife was not able to go to Kagoshima.

On January 14, 1862, Kichinosuke stayed in Anizaki port. Aikana brought Kikujiro by the hand. "I have refreshed myself by living with you. I will never forget your help."

"You have a great ambition. I believe your success." Kikujiro gazed at the great body of his father.

Many islanders sent Kichinosuke off. He arrived at Kagoshima on February 12. The next day Kichinosuke visited Hisamitsu, the father of the clan, in the second tower of Tsurumaru Castle.

Tadayoshi, the lord of the clan, was also there. Hisamitsu had been preparing to go to Kyoto. "What makes you go to Kyoto?" Kichinosuke asked Hisamitsu.

"Since imperial princes Kazunomiya married Shogun, my next work is to change the executive of the Shogunate." "Let me humbly say." "You hold immense political power in Satsuma."

"However, you have no special rank or title in Kyoto and Edo." "I think you should stop your plan of going to Kyoto."

「わしが西郷を呼び戻したのは、上洛の助けをもらうためじゃ。朝廷から幕政改革の勅許を頂く」

「久光様は、江戸では藩を代表する武士ではありませぬ。老中様が話を聞くはずはありませぬ」

「わしが田舎者だというのか」

「多くの藩士を率いて行くのですから、ここは忠義公が適役かと存じます」

忠義公は横で迷惑そうな顔をしている。

「上洛の準備は済んだ。3月13日には本隊が出発するので、西郷は村田と森山を連れて、2日前に下関に行き、待機せよ」

どこまでも筋論のわからぬ久光公にあきれて、吉之助は命令に従うことにした。

自宅に帰ってみると、肥後の宮部鼎蔵から手紙が来ていた。

その内容は、「宮部は全国で約2000名の倒幕派志士を集めたこと。薩摩の同志の合流を期待すること。2月末に来鹿するので話を聞いてもらいたいこと」であった。

吉之助は手紙をしたため、有馬新七に託した。有馬は西郷の代理として宮部に会い、手紙を渡し、情勢を聞いた。

"When we go to Kyoto, your help is necessary for Satsuma. Therefore, I recalled you to Kagoshima, I am going to gain the permission of the Court on the reform of the Shogunate."

"Mr. Hisamitsu you are not representative of the Satsuma clan in Edo. The principal retainers of the Shogunate shall never listen to your idea." "Do you mean I am just a fresh from the country?" "Because many samurais will be in command, I think Tadayoshi Shimazu, the lord of the clan, has suitable post."

Mr. Tadayoshi showed a look of annoyance. "The preparation for going to Edo has done. Our parade will start on March 13, So you Saigo should go to Shimonoseki and wait for me there with Murata and Moriyama two days before." To be disgusted Mr. Hisamitsu did not understand his logic a idea, Kichinosuke decided to obey the command. When Kichinosuke got home, a letter from Teizou Miyabe of the Higo clan arrived at Kichinosuke's home. The contents were as follows.

"Miyabe gathered about 2,000 of Jyoi samurais from around the nation. He has been expecting of Satsuma samurais to participate. When he come to Kagoshima in February, he want to see and talk with Kichinosuke." Kichinosuke passed his own letter for Miyabe to Shinshichi Arima and asked him to substitute for himself.

Arima met Miyabe instead of Saigo. And Arima gave the letter of Saigo to Miyabe.

Then he learned about the current national situation.

吉之助、村田、森山の3人は3月12日には下関に着いた。

　吉之助は二人を連れて白石正一郎宅を訪問した。白石氏は下関の豪商である。朝鮮、中国との密貿易で大もうけしたが、吉田松陰の弟子でもある。

　「奄美大島に3年もいたものですから、京都、江戸のことはなにもわかりません」。吉之助は白石に言った。

　「今回の久光公の上洛は攘夷を京都、江戸で決行するためで御座ろう。国民はそうみております」

　「いや、それは違いもす。幕政を改革するための圧力にすぎません」

　「薩摩の有馬新七様は先陣をきるため、兵を集めているそうですぞ」

　久光公に攘夷を決行する気が全くない事を吉之助は知っていた。今の薩摩の立場は幕府に睨まれ損をするだけである。

　「京に行き、有馬らの動きを止めることにする」

　吉之助一行は広島、赤穂を通り、姫城に着いていた。

　久光公が下関に着くと、吉之助一行がいないので、久光公は激怒した。

　「わしに無断で攘夷を決行するなど許さぬ」

　久光公は薩摩京都藩邸に着くと、鎮撫隊を結成し、吉之助の逮捕に乗り出した。

Three samurais, Kichinosuke Murata and Moriyama arrived at Shimonoseki on March 12. Kichinosuke accompanied by Murata and Moriyama visited the mansion of Shoichiro Shiraishi. Mr. Shiraishi was a wealthy merchant in Shimonoseki. He gained much money by smuggling with Korea and China. Also, he was a student of Shoin Yoshida in Shoin school.

"Because of the long stay for three years on Amami-Oshima island, I don't know the current situation of Kyoto and Edo." Kichinosuke said to Shiraishi. Shiraishi told about his own idea. "This visit to Kyoto of Hisamitsu, the father of the Satsuma clan, shall be the performance of exclusion of foreigners in Kyoto and Edo. It is natural most people are thinking so." "No, you are wrong. The idea of Hisamitsu is nothing but the pressure to reform the Shogunate and ministration." "I hear Shinshichi Arima has been gathering soldiers for the spear heading." Kichinosuke knew that Hisamitsu was never going to perform the exclusion of foreigners. The situation of the Satsuma clan was suspected of the performance of exclusion of foreigners by the Shogunate. His situation could have brought risk only. "We will go to Kyoto to stop the movement of Shinshichi Arima." Kichinosuke and two samurais had already arrived at Himeji castle by way of Hiroshima and Ako. Hisamitsu got very angry because of Kichinosuke's absence. "I never permit him to perform the exclusion of foreigners." As soon as Hisamitsu arrived at the Kyoto mansion of Satsuma, he planned to arrest Kichinosuke organizing suppression army.

3月29日、3人の武士は京都へ着いた。薩摩の多くの攘夷武士が藩邸に集まっていた。吉之助は村田と森山を連れて藩邸に入った。

　井伊直弼の死以来、攘夷の嵐が至る所で吹き荒れていた。しかし、攘夷を実行する者は誰もいなかった。吉之助は有馬に言った。

　「攘夷については急ぐことはない。なぜなら、久光公は攘夷の考えを持たないからだ。攘夷実行のためには大砲、軍艦、多くの兵を必要とする。あなた達は斉彬公の教えを忘れたのか。久光公は幕府改革を申し入れるために京都にきたのです」

　有馬は吉之助に激しく反論した。

　「我々が攘夷の先兵となるべきだ。なぜあなたは幕府と戦うのをためらうのか」

　吉之助は過激派を説得出来なかった。

　過激派の10人の武士が寺田屋に押しかけた。吉之助は久光公と会うのを避けるため、姫路へ帰ることを決心した。

　吉之助と他の2人の武士は久光公の送った鎮撫隊によって逮捕された。

　その後、有馬派と鎮撫隊の間で激しい戦闘が起きた。

　京都市民は久光公の弾圧政策を賞賛した。

On March 29, three samurais arrived at Kyoto. Many radical samurais of Satsuma gathered in the clan mansion. Kichinosuke entered the clan mansion with Murata and Moriyama. After the death of Naosuke Ii, the storm of exclusion of foreigners blew hard everywhere. However, nobody carry out the performance of exclusion of foreigners. Kichinosuke said to Arima. "You should not hurry about the exclusion of foreigners." "Because Hisamitu Shimzu has no idea of it." "We need big gun, war ship, and many soldiers for the performance of the exclusion of foreigners." "Why do you forget the teaching of Nariakira? Mr.Hsamitsu has come to Kyoto for proposal of the reform of the Shogunate." Arirna argued with Kichinosuke fiercely.

"We should be a pioneer of the exclusion of foreigners." "Why do you hesitate to fight with the Shogunate?" Kichinosuke could not persuade the radical group. To stop it, ten samurais of the radical group broke in Teradaya. Kichinosuke decided to return to Himeji to avoid collision to Hisamitsu.

Kichinosuke and other two samurais were arrested by the suppression army that was sent by Hisamitsu.

After that, the fierce battle broke out between Arima group and suppression army.

Kyoto citizens praised for the suppression policy of Hisamitsu.

第5章

　久光公は江戸で幕府の老中と会った。彼は3つの要求からなる書類を提出した。しかし、3つのうちでもっとも重きを置いた要求であった松平春嶽の大老就任を、幕府は拒絶した。

　久光公の一行は、江戸からの帰路、相模の生麦村で数人のイギリス人に邪魔された。薩摩武士がひとりのイギリス人を斬り殺した。その後、イギリス海軍が鹿児島市を砲撃した。

　文久2年（1862）8月18日には、薩摩藩と会津藩が京都において長州藩に勝利した。長州派の7人の公家は山口に逃げた。薩摩の隊長は高崎正風であった。薩摩の人気は急激に低下した。

　多くの京都市民は長州の勝利を望んでいた。

　文久2年（1862）7月2日、吉之助は徳之島の湾仁屋に着いた。村田新八は同じ頃、喜界島に着いた。山川から出発の朝、森山新蔵は自殺した。彼は寺田屋事件での息子、新五左衛門の死を深く嘆いていた。

　吉之助の徳之島滞在はわずか2カ月で、8月には沖永良部島に移された。

　2人の島役人と多くの島人が吉之助を迎えた。

　彼は馬に乗るのを勧められた。しかし、彼はこの申し出を断った。

Chapter 5

Mr.Hisamitsu met the principal retainers of the Shogunate. He submitted the documents consisted of three request. However, the shogunate rejected the promotion of Shungaku Matsudaira to the chief minister which was the main request. The parade of Hisamitsu was interfered by some English men in Namamugi village Sagami on the way back home from Edo. After that, English navy attacked Kagoshima city. On August 18, 1862, Satsuma clan and Aizu clan defeated the Choshu clan in Kyoto. The seven Court nobles belonging to Choshu group escaped to Yamaguchi. The leader of Satsuma was Seifu Takasaki. The popularity of Satsuma lost drastically. Many Kyoto citizens hoped the victory of Choshu.

On July 2, 1862, Kichinosuke arrived at Annia of Tokunoshima. Shinpachi Murata arrived at Kikaijima around the same. On the morning of this departure from Yamagawa, Shinzou Moriyama killed himself. He mourned the death of his son, Shingozaemon. Shingozaeraon had died in the Teradaya incident. Kichinosuke's stay on Tokunoshima was for only two month. In August, Kichinosuke was sent to Okinoerabu island. Two island officers and many islanders welcomed Kichinosuke. He was recommended riding a horse. But he refused this proposal.

吉之助は約2時間かけて歩いて牢に向かった。

牢は海岸から約10m離れた丘の上に立っていた。

松林の中に監視小屋があった。若い男が一人で住んでいた。彼は常に小さい小屋から吉之助を見ていた。

牢は雨、風、太陽、雷に晒されていた。風が強い時、海の波が牢に浸入した。

監視人の名前は土持正照であった。彼は一日に一回、吉之助に食べ物を運んだ。これは薩摩藩の規則であった。

彼は吉之助がその巨体のおかげで、大量の食べ物を摂ることに気が付いた。正照は生来優しい性格であった。彼は母が作った野菜を提供した。

正照は懸命に吉之助の世話をした。しかし、とうとう吉之助は病気になった。正照は代官の許可を得て、自費で座敷牢を作った。

正照は吉之助を座敷牢に移した。多くの子供達が新しい牢の前に集まった。吉之助は子供達にいろいろな学問を教えた。吉之助は正照と義兄弟となった。正照の母は涙を流して喜んだ。

「私はせごどんのお母さんよ。なんて嬉しいことなのこれは」

文久3年（1863）10月、吉之助の鹿児島への帰還が許された。

Kichinosuke went to the prison walking for about two hours. The prison stood on a hill ten meters far from the coast.

There was a watching house in a pine grove. A young man had been living by himself. He was always watching Kichinosuke from the small house. The prison was exposed to rain, wind, sun shine, and thunder. When it came the strong wind, the wave of ocean invaded the prison.

The name of watcher man was Masateru Tsuchimochi. He brought Kichinosuke foods once a day. This was the rule of the Satsuma clan. He noticed that Kichinosuke had to eat great quantity of meal due to his big body. Masateru had tender characteristic by nature. He served Kichinosuke vegetables which his mother had grown up.

Masateru took care of Kichinosuke sincerely. But, Kichinosuke became sick at last. Masateru made the straw mat prison at his own expense by mission of the local magistrate. Masateru moved Kichinosuke the straw mat prison. Many children gathered in front of new prison. Kichinosuke taught the children various learning. Kichinesuke became sworn brothers with Masateru. The mother of Masateru was pleased with tears of joy.

"I am the mother of Segodon! How happy this is." In October, 1863, Kichinosuke's return to Kagoshima was permitted.

吉之助は2月に鹿児島に帰ることを決めた。奄美群島では冬季の航海は大変危険であった。

　吉之助は役人の仕事と農業の重要性を正照に説いた。吉之助は島役人の就業心得を書き、正照に渡した。農業では、吉之助は穀物の保存のために高倉の活用を勧めた。

　吉之助は大久保から手紙を受け取った。手紙の概要は次の通りである。

　「公武合体は朝廷にとっては有利であった。なぜなら、和宮は孝明天皇の妹であった。それゆえ、天皇は将軍家茂に京都御所の警備を命じた。将軍は常に京都に滞在せねばならない。幕府は武家の政治を執行することができなかった。我々は朝廷と薩摩藩を繋ぐ人物を持っていない。その最も適当な人物は西郷吉之助であると私は考えている。私は久光公に私の考えを主張した」

　2月21日に、吉井友実と吉之助の弟西郷従道の乗った船が吉之助の帰還のために和泊港に入った。船は翌日龍郷に着いた。

　吉之助は二人の子供に会った。彼は赤子に菊子と名前を付けた。翌日、船は喜界島に着いた。

　村田新八が船に乗った。吉之助は新八の手を取って泣いた。

Kichinosuke decided to return to Kagoshima in February. In Amami islands, the voyage in winter season was so dangerous. Kichinosuke explained the work of officers and the promotion of agriculture to Masateru. Kichinosuke wrote about note to work as island officers and Masateru this document. In agriculture, Kichinosuke taught recommended him to construct and make good use of a high warehouse for the preservation of grains. Kichinosuke received the letter from Okubo. The summary of his letter was as follows.

"The policy of union of the Imperial court and the Shogunate was advantageous for the Court. Because Kazunomiya was younger sister of the Emperor Komei. The Emperor Komei ordered Shogun Iemochi to guard Kyoto Imperial palace. The Shogunate was not able to execute the politics of samurai. We have no person unite the Court and Satsuma clan. I think that the most suitable person is Kichinosuke Saigo. I have affirmed about my idea to Mr. Hisamitsu."

On February 21, the ship of Tomozane Yoshii and Tsugumichi Saigo, Kichinosuke's younger brother entered Wadomari port for the return of Kichinosuke. The ship arrived at Tatsugo the next day. Kichinosuke met two children. He named his baby girl Kikuko. The next day, the ship arrived at Kikaijima island.

Shinpachi Murata boarded the ship. Kichinosuke shed tears, taking Shinpachi.

第6章

　元治元年（1864）3月14日、吉之助は村田と共に京都に到着した。彼は薩摩軍の陸軍司令官に任命された。
　前年、薩摩藩は桜町御門で長州藩に勝利していた。
　吉之助は京都に着いた時、薩摩藩の不人気に驚いた。会津、長州、京都市民が薩摩藩を嫌っていた。吉之助は京都御所の警備に専念した。
　この年の6月、新撰組が29名の攘夷武士を池田屋事件で殺した。松陰の門下生、吉田稔麿が新撰組に殺された。長州兵が続々と京都市内に集まった。
　吉之助は京都丹後の桜揮楼で会議を開いた。
　「国父久光公は長州への攻撃を命じた」
　「我々は長州と戦う。しかし、会津に頼ってはならない」
　「おそらく、蛤御門が最後の戦場となるだろう」
　「我々の守るべき場所は乾御門である。しかし、我々は最終段階で蛤御門に侵入するつもりである。我々は長州兵を追い出さねばならない」吉之助は要点を述べた。
　長州兵は8月18日の政変以来、山口に追われた。しかし、長州のいくらかの兵士は秘密裏に活動していた。朝廷はなお攘夷を主張していた。幕府は攘夷を実行できなかった。

Chapter 6

On March 14, Kichinosuke arrived at Kyoto with Murata. He was appointed to the commander of the Satsuma army. On the previous year, Satsuma clan defeated the Choshu clan in Sakuramachi gate. When Kichinosuke arrived at Kyoto, he was surprised at the unpopularity with the Satsuma clan. Aizu, Choshu and Kyoto citizens hated Satsuma. Kichinosuke engaged in protecting Kyoto Imperial palace. In June of the year, Shinsengumi killed 29 samurais of exclusionists in Ikedaya incident. Toshimaro Yoshida, a disciple of Shoin, was killed by Shinsengumi. Choshu soldiers gathered at Kyoto city one after another. Kichinosuke has a meeting at Okiro in Tango, Kyoto. "The father of the clan, Hisamitsu, ordered us to attack Choshu." "We are going to battle against Choshu. But, we never depend on Aizu." "Perhaps Hamagurigomon gate shall be the last battlefield." "Inui gate is the place we should defend. But we are going to invade Hamagurigomon gate in the last stage." "We must drive out Choshu soldiers."

Kichinosuke told the important points. Choshu soldiers had been driven away Yamaguchi after the revolusion of August 18. However some members of Choshu has been acting in secret. The Court had been still insisting the policy of Jyoi, exclusion of foreigners. The Shogunate could not perform the exclusion of foreigners.

長州藩主、毛利敬親は公職を奪われていた。

　そして、彼は長州藩邸に謹慎していた。長州藩は難しい立場にあった。益田、福原、国司の３家老は積極策を提案した。それは孝明天皇に長州の正当性を訴えることであった。一方、高杉晋作は慎重な考えを提案した。

　最後の結論として、長州藩は京都に兵を送った。

　長州藩は京都の入り口、天王山に本陣を置いた。兵の数はおよそ600であった。

　益田親施、久坂玄瑞と他の浪人が戦闘を待っていた。

　福原越後は長州藩の伏見藩邸に800の兵を持っていた。長州軍は孝明天皇に嘆願書を提出した。その内容は次の通りである。

　　長州藩主の京都滞在の許可

　　長州派の５人の公家の京都滞在の許可

　　攘夷政策の確立

　しかし、孝明天皇はこれらの要求を拒絶した。

　彼は京都からの長州軍の撤退を命じた。

　およそ1000人の薩摩兵が京都に到着した。徳川慶喜はいくつかの藩が出兵することを命じた。大垣藩と桑名藩が幕府軍に加入した。幕府軍の総兵力は約６万に増加した。

The lord of the Choshu clan, Takachika Mouri had been robed his official post and confined in Choshu clan mansion. The Choshu clan was on a tough situation. Three principal retainers Masuda, Fukuhara and Kokushi proposed a positive policy. It was to appeal Emperor Komei the justice of Choshu. On the other hand, Shinsaku Takasugi proposed prudence idea. As the last decision, Choshu clan sent soldiers to Kyoto.

The Choshu clan put the headquarters on Tennouzan the entrance of Kyoto. The number of soldiers was about 600. Chikashi Masuda, Genzui Kusaka and other ronin had been waiting for a battle. Echigo Fukuhara had 800 of soldiers in Fushimi mansion of the Choshu clan. The Choshu army submitted Emperor Komei a petition. Its contents were as follows.

The permission for the lord of the Choshu clan to stay in Kyoto. The permission for the five Court nobles of Choshu group to stay in Kyoto.

Establishment of the policy of the exclusion of foreigners.

However, Emperor Komei rejected these request. He ordered of Choshu army to withdraw from Kyoto. About 1,000 of soldiers of Satsuma arrived at Kyoto. Yoshinobu Tokugawa ordered that some clans should sent soldiers. The Ogaki clan and Kuwana clan joined the Shogunate army. Total military of the Shogunate increased to about 60,000.

不利な状況にもかかわらず、長州の久坂玄瑞は各藩に手紙を送った。

　長州軍の軍議は不利な戦況のもとで行われた。

　孝明天皇は長州軍の撤退を命じた。

　「我々は長州へ逃げるべきです」。久坂は言った。

　「なぜこの段階で君は幕府を攻撃するのをためらうのか。命を惜しんではならぬ」

　急進派の来島又兵衛は久坂に言った。最古参の侍和泉真木の同意により、久坂は自分の本営に戻った。

　久坂は松陰の松下村塾で抜群の秀才と言われた。松陰なきあと、高杉晋作、吉田稔麿らと尊皇攘夷運動を推進した。

　彼はどちらかといえば穏健派で、倒幕のための挙兵は時期尚早と考えていた。過激派の３家老への恩義があり、京都へ来てしまった。頼みの綱は孝明天皇であった。

　薩摩の大軍が入京し、幕府側につき、天皇はついに長州の京都撤退を命じた。

　長州はわずか3000の兵で６万の幕府、会津、薩摩の兵と戦う情勢となった。

In spite of the disadvantaged situation, Genzui Kusaka of Choshu submitted the letter to each clan. The meeting of the Choshu army was hold in disadvantageous war condition.

Emperor Komei ordered our army to withdraw.

"We should escape to Choshu." Kusaka said.

"Why do you hesitate to attack the Shogunate in this stage. Never cling to your life."

Matabei Kurushima of the radical group said to Kusaka. By agreement of Izumi Maki, who was the oldest senior samurai, Kusaka returned to his own camp. Kusaka was evaluated as an outstanding bright student in the shokasonjuku which Shoin Yoshida managed. He promoted Jyoi movement with Shinsaku Takasugi and Toshimaro Yoshida after the death of Shoin. As he was in a moderate group, he had been thinking that making an army to attack the Shogunate was too early. Since he felt greatful for three clan retainer, he had no choice except going to Kyoto. Emperor Komei was his last hope. The big army of Satsuma arrived at Kyoto. Owing to the join of Satsuma to the Shogunate, the Emperor ordered the Choshu army to withdraw.

The Choshu army had to battle by only of 3,000 of soldiers towards 60,000 of soldiers consist of the Shogunate, Aizu and Satsuma.

第7章

　朝廷における長州派は、8月政変で山口に送られた7人の公家以外にも数人がいた。これらの公家は反対勢力として逃亡すると考えられてきた。

　孝明天皇の弟、有栖川宮は長州派に属していた。彼は松平容保を追放することを主張した。

　この情報は徳川慶喜に報告された。慶喜は馬に乗って朝廷に行った。慶喜は長州追放の勅許を得た。

　京都御所には多くの門があった。薩摩軍は乾御門を守っていた。蛤御門は多くの会津兵によって守られていた。

　長州と幕府の最後の交渉は決裂した。

　元治元年（1864）7月19日、福原越後率いる800の兵が公家鷹司卿の邸宅を攻撃し始めた。藤森神社に駐在する長州藩は大垣藩の大砲によって攻撃された。福原越後は顔に怪我をした。福原軍は宝塔寺で敗北した。長州軍は山崎と竹田街道で、新撰組の近藤勇と土方歳三に敗北した。

　天龍寺の来島隊は突然、蛤御門へ移動した。

　会津軍は長州軍と激しく戦った。

　突然、薩摩軍が会津軍を助けるために現れた。吉之助は左手に高々と長刀を上げた。

Chapter 7

Choshu groups in the Court had some persons except seven Court nobles who were sent to Yamaguchi in political change of August. It had been said that these Court nobles would go off an opposing power. Arisugawanomiya, younger brother of Emperor Komei belonged to Choshu group. He persisted in banishing Katamori Matsudaira. This information was reported to Yoshinobu Tokugawa. Yoshinobu went to Court riding a horse. Yoshinobu gained the Imperial sanction for Choshu banishment.

Kyoto Imperial palace had many gate. Satsuma army had been defending Inui gate. Hamagurigomon gate was guarded by many Aizu samurais. The last negotiation of Choshu and the Shogunate was broken down.

On July 19, 1864, 800 soldiers of Echigo Fukuhara army began to attack the mansion of Court noble Takatsukasa. The Choshu clan staying at Fujimori Temple was attacked by big guns of Ogaki clan. Echigo Fukuhara was injured in the face. Fukuhara group was defeated at Hotoji Temple. Choshu army was defeated by Isami Kondo and Toshizo Hijikata of Shinsengumi on Yamasaki and Takeda road. Kurushima group of Tenryuji moved to Hamagurigomon gate suddenly. Aizu army battled with Choshu army fiercely. Suddenly Satsuma army appeared to help Aizu army. Kichinosuke raised his long sword highly in his left hand.

そして、彼は叫んだ。「前へ進め。下がってはならぬ」

吉之助の大きな目は最初から最後までぎらぎら光っていた。「あの大きな男が薩摩の西郷だ。」

長州兵は吉之助に狙いを絞った。吉之助は左手に軽い傷を受けた。5人の薩摩兵が吉之助の盾となって倒れた。長州の来島又兵衛は薩摩兵の槍によって心臓を刺された。彼は大きな痛みの中にあった。

「どうか、私の首を討ってくれ」。彼は仲間から介錯を受けた。一方、真木和泉と久坂玄瑞は天王山の本営から船出した。

桂川の船の中で、真木と久坂は来島の死と福原越後軍の崩壊を知った。真木と久坂は京都御所の桜町御門を攻撃した。

攻撃の後、真木、久坂、寺島忠三郎は公家、鷹司卿の屋敷に侵入した。長州の3人の武士は朝廷へ嘆願書を提出しようと試みた。

しかし、鷹司邸は会津兵に包囲された。久坂と寺島は公家鷹司卿に嘆願書を渡すことができず、この2人の侍は自分の首を斬ることにより自分の生涯を終えた。松陰の優れた弟子、久坂は不運な生涯を終えた。

真木和泉は天王山へ逃げた。しかし、彼は会津藩と新撰組との戦いで戦死した。長州兵の265名が戦死した。

And he cried. "Go forward." "Never move back." Big eyes of Kichinosuke were glittering from the first to the last. "That big man is Saigo of Satsuma." Snipe shooting of Choshu soldiers aimed at Kichinosuke.

Kichinosuke was injured on left hand slightly. Five Satsuma soldiers fell down as the sacrifice of Kichinosuke. Matabei Kurushima of Choshu was attacked on his heart with a spear of of Satsuma soldiers. He was in great pain. "Please cut down my neck." He had a comparison cut off his head. On the other hand, Izumi Maki and Genzui Kusaka sallied from the camp of Tennozan.

On a ship in Katsuragawa, Maki and Kusaka knew the death of Krushima and the collapse of Echigo Fukuhara army. Maki and Kusaka attacked Sakuramachi gate of Kyoto grand palace. After the attack, Maki, Kusaka and Chuzaburo Terashima invaded the mansion of noble Takatsukasa. Three samurais of Choshu tried to submit petition to the Court. However, Takatsukasa mansion was surrounded by Aizu soldiers. Kusaka and Terashima were not able to take petition to the Court noble Takatsukasa. Both samurais ended in killing the own neck. Bright pupil of Shoin, Kusaka ended his unfortunate life. Izumi Maki escaped to Tennozan. Hewever, he died by the attack of Aizu clan and Shinsengumi. 265 of Choshu soldiers were killed.

吉之助は銃の使用が禁止されている京都御所の勅令を守り、槍と刀で突進し、会津兵を蛤御門から追い払った。そして、銃で応戦する長州兵に勝利した。戦闘は1日で終わったが、吉之助は軍神として恐れられるようになった。

　前年の8月政変の後、京都における薩摩の評判は極度に悪くなっていた。薩摩の商人が密貿易で儲けて、さらに清国、琉球国から仕入れた商品を京都、大阪で販売し、物価をつり上げていた。吉之助は薩摩出身の商人の帰国を命じた。

　吉之助が流刑に処せられていた1年7カ月の間に、久光公が音頭をとった公武合体政策は矛盾と行き詰まりに直面していた。6月5日の池田屋で、長州、肥後等の活動家29名が死亡した事件で、新撰組を応援したのは会津藩であり、会津藩は京都市民に憎まれていた。

　人民に尊敬される役人であることが、政治、行政では重要であることを、吉之助は5年間の流刑生活で学んでいた。

　大藩である薩摩、長州が手を組むことを京都市民は望んでいた。それを早くから知っていたのは坂本龍馬である。

　龍馬は京都の薩摩藩邸でもある小松帯刀邸に吉之助をたびたび訪問し、薩長連合の必要を説いた。

Kichinosuke obeyed the rule of Kyoto Imperial Palace where the shooting of guns had been prohibited. And he charged at Hamaguri gate using spear and a sword and drove away Aizu soldiers. He gained the victory over the Choshu clan army attacking with a gun. Although the battle ended in a day, Kichinosuke came to be feared of the power as he is god of a war. After political change of August of the previous year, the reputation ef Satsuma in Kyoto became the worst. A merchant of Satsuma had been gaining big profit in smuggling. And they sold merchandise from sin kingdom and Ryukyu kingdom in Kyoto and Osaka. These activity contributed to rise in price. Kichinosuke ordered that these merchants should return to Kagoshima. While the 19 month of Kichinosuke's exile, the policy of the reconciliation between the Court and the Shogunate that Hisamitsu had been promoting, had faced inconsistency and deadlock. In Ikedaya incident of June 5, Shinsengumi killed 29 samurais of Choshu and Higo. Due to the Aizu clan's suport for them, this incident was performed. Kyoto citizens hated Aizu samurais. It is important for officers to be loved from the people on politics and administration. Kichinosuke had learned by this truth from his five years's exile.

The citizen of Kyoto had hoped that Satsuma and Choshu of big clans would unite. Ryoma Sakamoto had realized for a long time. Ryoma visited Kichinosuke at Satsuma clan mansion of Tatewaki Komatsu. Ryoma explained the alliance of Satsuma and Choshu.

9月11日、吉之助は福井藩士の紹介で幕臣の勝海舟と会った。勝は率直で歯切れの良い江戸っ子で、博識であった。幕府の内情をざっくばらんに話してくれた。勝は幕府に人材がいないことをみずから話した。

　龍馬と勝の話を聞き、吉之助は倒幕を真剣に考えるようになった。

　しかし、薩摩には藩論を統一してから実行に移すという伝統があり、条約破棄と攘夷へ方針を転換するのは容易ではなかった。

　蛤御門の変後、長州は朝敵となり、幕府は長州征伐の軍を編成した。征長軍の総督には尾張藩主徳川慶勝、参謀には西郷吉之助が任命された。慶勝は吉之助に尾張藩の宝刀を下賜して全権を委任した。将軍後見人の徳川慶喜は吉之助が長州藩を壊滅してくれることを望んでいた。しかし、吉之助には長州藩を潰すという了見はなかった。

　吉之助は岩国藩の吉川賢物と会談し、２つの降伏条件を示した。

　　１　蛤御門の変の首謀者である３家老と４参謀の処罰。
　　２　文久３年（1863）８月政変で長州に逃れた５卿の動座（他藩に移すこと）。

On September 11, Kichinosuke met an executlve of the Shogunate, Kaisyu Katsu, with an introduction from a samurai the Fukui clan. Katsu was a frank and smart Edo-style person. He had vast knowledge. Katsu told frankly about the situation of the Shogunate and explained that the Shogunate had no talented persons. Kichinosuke came to think of the collapse of the Shogunate after listening to Ryoma and Katsu.

However, there was the tradition of Satsuma that the performance should be carried out after the several discussions and unified the view in the Satsuma clan. Therefore, it was so difficult to change the policy for another that was the cancel of the treaty and the performance of Jyoi. After of Hamagurigomon gate incident, Choshu clan became the enemy of the Court. The Shogunate made the arm of the conquest of Choshu.

Yoshikatsu Tokugawa was appointed as the general of the army. Kichinosuke Saigo was appointed as the top staff officer. Yoshikatsu invested Kichinosuke with full power, giving the treasured swords of the Owari clan. Yoshinobu Tokugawa, guardian of the shogun, hoped that Kichinosuke would defeat the Choshu clan. However, kichinosuke had no idea of collapsing the Choshu clan. Kichinosuke met Kenmotsu Kikkawa of the Iwaki clan and Kichinosuke showed two terms of surrender. They were as follows.

1. Harakiri of the three principal retainers and the death penalties of the four staff officers, the leader in Hamagurigomon gate incident.

2. Transfer movements of the five Court officers of Choshu groups escaping into choshu in political change of August in 1863.

吉川は条件を受け入れ、3家老の切腹と4参謀の斬首を実行した。しかし、5卿動座には長州藩内で奇兵隊を中心とした反対運動が起きた。5卿を確保しておくことは、長州藩が勤王藩として働いてきた証拠だからである。

　吉之助は1人で長州に出かけて、交渉することにした。

　桐野、村田らは驚いて反対をした。しかし、吉之助は突然長州藩諸隊を訪問した。

　吉之助は内戦をおこしてはならない、5卿を他藩に移せば征長軍を解体できる、と説き、長州軍を納得させた。

　翌年の元治2年（1865）1月15日、5卿は筑前太宰府に移された。16日に徳川慶勝は大阪城に行き、征長軍の解散を命じた。

　一方、吉之助は鹿児島に帰り、国父久光、藩主忠義に長州との連合、倒幕の必要性を説明した。

　吉之助が5卿問題で長州で奮闘していた頃、坂本龍馬、大久保利通、小松帯刀は吉之助の縁談を進めていた。

　元治2年（1865）1月28日、吉之助は岩山糸子と結婚した。披露宴には国父久光公も出席し、祝いの言葉を述べた。

Kenmotsu Kikkawa accepted the surrender condition and he performed Harakiri of the three principal retainers and the death penalties of the four staff officers. On the purge of five court nobles. the opposite movement by Kiheitai happened in the Choshu clan.

To have the five Court nobles was the evidence that Choshu clan had been working for the Court. Kichinosuke decided to go to Choshu by himself for the negotiation on transfer of the five Court nobles. Kirino and Murata opposed Kichinosuke's going to Kyoto. But, Kichinosuke visited each army of Choshu suddenly. Kichinosuke said to the captain of each army. "You must not begin a civil war." "We are able to demolish the union army by the transfer of the five Court nobles."

Choshu soldiers understood Kichinosuke's idea. On January 15 1865, the five Court nobles of Choshu group moved to Dazaifu. On January 16, Yoshikatsu Tokugawa went to Osaka Castle and he ordered the dismissal of the army of conquest of Choshu.

On the other hand, Kichinosuke went back to Kagoshima. And he explained the necessity of alliance with Choshu and overthrow of the Shogunate to Hisamitsu and Tadayoshi. When Kichinosuke was acting to Choshu for the transfer of the five Court nobles, Ryoma,Okubo and Tatewaki Komatsu were processing the marriage of Kichinosuke. On January 28, 1865, Kichinosuke married Itoko Iwayama. The father of the clan, Hisamitsu attended the wedding ceremony and he made a congratulatory speech.

慶応元年（1865）3月9日には朝廷が幕府に参勤交代をゆるめよと指示を出すに至り、幕府の権威の衰えは誰の目にも明らかとなった。4月7日には孝明天皇の病気悪化により、皇太子が政務を執るようになり、慶応と改元された。
　幕府は長州再討伐の計画を立て、各藩の部署を定めた。
　坂本龍馬は馬関で木戸孝允と会見し、薩摩、長州の和解を図った。土佐の中岡慎太郎は鹿児島に行き、吉之助に長州との和解を斡旋した。
　一方、幕府は将軍家茂自ら長州再征伐を朝廷に申し入れし勅許を得たが、開港の許可は得られなかった。
　長州は禁門の変で朝敵となり、窮地に陥っていた。一方薩摩は、幕政改革の展望が見いだせず、対幕府強硬論が高まっていた。ここに両者の利害が一致することとなった。
　慶応2年（1866）1月21日、薩摩藩の小松帯刀邸で坂本龍馬の立ち会いのもとで、薩長の同盟が締結された。
　この同盟は6箇条からなるが、共同で倒幕へ動くという内容ではなく、長州藩の状況が悪くなっても、薩摩藩は長州を支援するという内容であった。

In March 9, 1865, the Court ordered the Shogunate to weaken the system of alternative attendance. Everybody realized the weakness of authority of the Shogunate. On April 7, the era name changed from Ganji to Keio because the new Crown Prince started to govern due to a disease of Emperor Komei. The Shogunate made the plan of the second conquest of Choshu and shogun appointed the post of each clan.

Ryoma Sakamoto met Takayoshi Kido in Bakan and attempted the reconciliation between Satsuma and Choshu. Shintaro Nakaoka from Toba went to Kagoshima and offered Saigo to act an intermediary between Satsuma and Choshu.

On the other hand, Iemochi the shogun proposed the Court for the second conquest of Choshu and gained the permission of the Court. They were in cornered. On the other hand, Satsuma clan could not find the views of the Shogunate government reform.

The number of hard-liners against the Shogunate was increasing more and more.

Then two clans discovered a conformity of interest at last. On January 21, 1866, the Satsuma-Choshu alliance was formed in the presence of Ryoma Sakamoto on the mansion of Tatewaki Komatsu of the Satsuma clan.

This alliance consisted of six items. The contents were not overthrow of the Shogunate in cooperation, but Satsuma's constant support for Choshu in the case of the tight situation.

第8章

　同盟の内容は記録されなかった。

　長州の木戸は後日龍馬に確認事項を記載した書簡を送った。龍馬はこの確認事項の文書に間違いはないと朱書して、木戸に返書した。

　この文書は第2次長州征伐に際し、薩摩が長州に対し、物心両面で援助を約束したものである。

　　第1条、長州で戦争が始まった場合、薩摩が京都、大阪に出兵して幕府に圧力を加えること。

　　第2条〜第4条、戦争の結果如何に関わらず、薩摩は長州の政治的復権のため、朝廷工作を行うこと。

　　第5条、薩摩が畿内に出兵したとき、幕府が朝廷を牛耳り、薩摩の要求を拒むなら、薩摩が幕府に軍事的に対決することを、長州側に表明すること。

　以上が薩摩長州同盟の内容である。

　太宰府滞在の5卿の京都帰還を幕府が要求するのは当然なので、吉之助は大山格之助と黒田清隆を太宰府に派遣し、5卿を守らせた。

Chapter 8

No the contents of alliance were recorded. Takayoshi Kido sent Ryoma Sakamoto the documents that recorded confirmation items on alliance meeting. Ryoma sent Kido this documents that were written by red pencil as the contents is accurate. This documents was that Satsuma promised Choshu to give assistance both physically and mentally.

Article 1: In the case of the war of Choshu towards the Shogunate, Satsuma give the Shogunate a pressure by sending soldiers to Kyoto and Osaka.

Article 2 to Article 4: Regardless of the result of the war, Satsuma must effort to change the Court for the political regain of Choshu.

Artide 5: When Satsuma send soldiers to Kinki district, if the Court and the Shogunate reject the request of Satsuma, Satsuma should fight against the Shogunate.

The above-mentioned items were the contents of the alliance. It was natural that the Shogunate request the return of five Court officers.

Therefore, Kichinosuke ordered Kakunosuke Oyama and Kiyotaka Kuroda the protect of five Court officers.

第9章

　6月5日、将軍家茂は大阪城に入り、長征の本営とした。幕府は32藩に出兵を命じ約15万の兵を集めた。幕府軍は大島、芸州、石州、小倉の四方から長州に攻め入った。武器は槍と刀であった。長州は海に軍艦を浮かべ、領内の大砲と銃で応戦した。

　薩摩は長州と同盟を結んでいたが、薩英戦争で街を焼かれ、戦費もなかったので、参戦しなかった。

　幕府は緒戦から敗戦続きであった。大きな原因は武器の差であった。

　結局、将軍家茂の死を理由に幕府は撤兵した。

　慶喜は、本意ではなかったが、7月29日に将軍職を受諾した。

　吉之助は幕府の大政奉還は必至とみて、小松帯刀と共に兵を率いて上京した。

　10月3日、土佐藩は単独で、大政奉還の建白書を藩主山内豊範を通じ将軍徳川慶喜に提出した。

　土佐藩の建白書を受け、10月13日、徳川慶喜は上洛中の重臣に大政奉還を諮問した。

　吉之助や土佐藩の後藤象二郎の働きかけにより、慶喜を加えた朝議により大政奉還が決定した。

　しかし、慶喜は将軍職の辞任と領地の返納にはふれていなかったので、吉之助は慶喜の将軍辞任を要求した。

Chapter 9

On June 5, the shogun Iemochi entered Osaka Castle. And he designated this castle as main office of the conquest of Choshu. The Shogunate ordered 32 of the clan to send soldiers. About 150,000 of soldiers gathered. The Shogunate army invaded Choshu territory from four directions of Oshima, Geishu, Sekishu and Kokura. Their arms were spears and swords. The Choshu clan fought using warships, big guns and short guns. Although Satsuma clan united the war alliance with the Choshu clan, they did not participate in the war due to little money. The Shogunate had been defeated since the first stage. The main reason was the weakness of weapons. In the result, the Shogunate army escaped from Choshu. Kichinosuke went to Kyoto with Tatewaki Komatsu knowing unavoidable situation of the transfer of political power back to the Emperor.

On October 3, the Tosa clan submitted Yoshinobu Tokugawa the written memorial of transfer of political power back to the Emperor through the lord of the Tosa clan, Toyonori Yamanouchi. After receiving the written memorial, Yoshinobu Tokugawa inquired of the main Daimyo staying Kyoto about the transfer of political power on October 13.

Owing to the pressure of Kichinosuke and Shojiro Goto of Tosa, the permission of the Court for the transfer of power back to the Emperor was given by the Court meeting containing Yoshinobu. However, Yoshinobu had no comment on the resignation of the Shogun post and the return of the own territory. Kichinosuke requested the resignation of the Shogun.

吉之助、大久保、小松は久光の了解を得た上で、武力倒幕路線に転換した。慶喜は倒幕の密勅が出される寸前に大政を奉還した。

　慶応3年（1867）12月9日未明、薩摩藩など5藩の軍が御所9門を固め、王政復古の大号令が発せられた。

　この大号令の後、新設の3職（総裁、議定、参与）を小御所へ召集し、小御所会議が開かれた。明治天皇のほか、総裁の有栖川宮、議定の仁和寺宮ら10名、参与は公家と地方武士16名であった。

　薩摩からは議定の島津忠義、参与の岩下方平、西郷吉之助、大久保利通であった。

　明治天皇の外祖父議定中山忠能が開会を宣言した。

　公家側から「慶喜は政権を返上したが、内大臣の官位と600万石の領地も返還すべきである」という議題が上程された。

　これに対し土佐の山内容堂は「この会議に功績のある慶喜公を出席させなかったのは陰険である。公家が若い天皇を利用して権力を盗もうとしている」とのべた。

　公家で参与の岩倉具視は「今日の会議は新天皇の決断による開催である」と反論した。

Kichinosuke, Okubo and Komatsu changed the clan policy into the overthrow of the Shogunate with the permission of Hisamitsu. Yoshinobu returned the political power just before the issue of the secret order. On the early morning of December 9, 1867, the big command of the Restoration was emitted in Kyoto city after Satsuma and other four clans protected nine gate of Kyoto Imperial Palace. After the big command, established three posts, president, minister, and councilor gathered small Imperial palace. The meeting was held there. The attendants were as follows.

The Emperor Meiji, Arisugawanomiya of president, 10 minister contained Ninnajinomiya, 16 councilors contained Kichinosuke Saigo. There were attendants of four clans, Tadayoshi Shimazu, Yoshihira Iwashita, Kichinosuke Saigo and Toshimichi Okubo from the Satsuma clan.

Tadanori Nakayama, maternal grandfather of the Emperor Meiji and one of ministers declared the opening of the meeting. Some Court officers proposed the subject.

"Although Yoshinobu returned the political power, he must return the territory of 6,000,000 goku."

Yodo Yamanouchi, the lord of the Tosa clan, said on this item.

"It is so crafty that former Shogun Yoshinobu was made to absent from this meeting." "Court officers are going to rob the political power by utilizing young Emperor."

Tomomi Iwakura of councilor said. "Today's meeting was opened by the new Emperor."

第10章

　小御所会議では総裁、議定、参与の３職が決まり、将軍の辞任と領地返納がきまった。ところが、新政府の設立が決まったわけではないので、慶喜は領地の返納を実行しなかった。幕府の天領はそのままなので、代官はそのまま職に留まった。慶喜は日本を代表して外交を行った。

　慶喜は明治天皇のいる京都を離れ、大阪城に移った。大阪城には幕府の旗本、佐幕派の藩兵１万2000がいた。小御所会議では尾張、越前、広島、土佐の大藩の４候が主導権を握り、参与である西郷、大久保などの地方武士は発言を抑えられた。慶喜の思惑どおりに事態は推移した。吉之助はここで奇策に打ってでた。

　江戸にいる薩摩出身の浪人達に江戸城、旗本屋敷への放火を命令したのである。

　江戸城の火事はすぐに消されたが、旗本屋敷の火事は浅草の商店街に広がり、江戸は大騒ぎとなった。

　放火の犯人が薩摩人と分かると大阪城の旗本、会津兵は烈火の如く怒り、慶喜は暴発を止めることは出来なかった。慶喜は一橋家に養子に入ったので、自分の譜代の家臣をほとんど持たなかった。

Chapter 10

At the meeting of small Imperial Palace, the three posts, president, minister, and councilor were decided. Also, the resignation and the return of the territory of the shogun were decided. On the other hand, as the establish of the new government was not decided, Yoshinobu did not carry out the return of his own territory. As the territory was left without any change, the chief magistrates was still working under the former condition. Yoshinobu performed diplomacy as the representative politician of Japan.

Yoshinobu left Kyoto where the Emperor Meiji were staying and moved to Osaka Castle. There were 12,000 of direct retainer of Shogun and samurai of various clans. As the meeting of small Imperial Palace four lords of the big clans, Owari, Echizen, Tosa, and Hiroshima took the advantage. The local samurais such as Kichinosuke and Okubo could not show their own thoughts. The situation moved as the strategy of Yoshinobu. When things had gone this far, Kichinosuke operated an ingenious scheme. He ordered fire-raising on Edo Castle and mansions of the direct retainers of Shogun to masterless Satsuma samurais living in Edo. The fire of Edo Castle was put out instantly. The fire of the mansion of the direct retainers spread to the shopping area of Asakusa. Edo was in uproar. As soon as it were found to had been broken out by Satsuma samurais, soldiers of Osaka Castle were in great anger. Yoshinobu could not stop their anger. Yoshinobu had no retainers from his father. Because he was the adopted son of the Hitotsubashi family.

慶応4年（1868）1月1日、慶喜は討薩の表を発表し、翌日から京都封鎖を目的とした出兵を開始した。

旧幕府の歩兵、桑名藩、見廻組は鳥羽街道を進んだ。会津藩、新撰組は伏見を目指した。

旧幕府軍の蜂起を受けて、朝廷は彦根藩と在京の藩に大津への出兵を命じた。大津に来たのは大村藩の50名であった。

1月3日、朝廷では緊急会議が招集された。

参与である大久保と西郷吉之助が旧幕府軍の入京は大号令への違反であると主張した。

議定の松平春嶽は旧幕府軍の出兵は薩摩藩への攻撃であり、朝廷は無関係であると主張した。

会議は紛糾したが、議定の岩倉が徳川征討に賛成したことにより、徳川征討が決まった。

島津斉彬は存命中、天保山の海岸で離合集散の明瞭な洋式の銃撃訓練をしていた。薩摩は実戦で有効な自顕流剣法でも有名であった。

鳥羽街道を進んできた旧幕府軍先鋒と薩摩軍の銃兵隊が激突した。吉之助は鶴翼の陣を作り、スナイドル銃で旧幕府軍に弾幕掃射を浴びせた。桑名藩砲兵隊も反撃したが、薩摩藩兵の優勢な銃撃の前に死傷者を増やし、ついに下鳥羽方面に退却した。

On January first, 1868, Yoshinobu Tokugawa announced the Satsuma sweeping program. The old Shogunate began to send soldiers for the purpose of the blockade on Kyoto. Infantry of the old Shogunate soldiers of the Kuwana clan and Mimawarigumi* advanced on Toba road. The Aizu clan and Shinsengumi went to ward Fushimi. With revolt of the old Shogunate army, the Court ordered that the Hikone clan and some clans staying kyoto should send soldiers to Otsu. Only 50 of soldiers came to Otsu.

On January 3, the emergency meeting was held in the Court. Ichizo Okubo and Kichinosuke Saigo affirmed that the entering kyoto of the old Shogunate army was the violation against the big command of Restoration. The meeting was confused. But, as Iwakura agreed to banish Tokugawa, the suppress of Tokugawa army was decided. Nariakira Shimazu had trained gun shooting in the western style of meeting and parting on the beach of Tenpozan. The Satsuma clan was famous for its sword technique of Jigenryu.

The vanguard of the old Shogunate army and gun soldiers of Satsuma crashed on Toba-Kaido road. Kichinosuke made a battle formation of wings of a crane. Satsuma soldiers attacked the old Shogunate soldiers by horizontal shooting of Snider gun. Though gun soldiers of the Kuwana clan fought back, gun shooting of Satsuma had the advantage. And the number of dead persons was increasing. At last, soldiers of the Kuwana clan escaped to Shimotoba.

*Mimawarigumi:a group for the security of Kyoto

一方、伏見では、伏見奉行所は陸軍奉行竹中の指揮する旧幕府軍と新撰組によって守られた。

　薩摩と長州の連合軍800人は、奉行所を包囲する形で布陣した。奉行所内の会津藩兵と新撰組が包囲を破ろうとして斬り込みをかけたが、高台に布陣していた薩摩藩兵が会津に砲撃と銃撃を加えた。

　薩摩藩の大砲の砲弾が奉行所内の弾薬庫に命中し、奉行所は炎上した。

　新政府軍は周囲の民家に放火しながら銃撃した。旧幕府軍は退去し、奉行所は新政府軍に占領された。

　近江方面では譜代の大藩、彦根藩が新政府軍に加入した。

　1月4日には、鳥羽方面で旧幕府軍が一時盛り返した。

　しかし、指揮官の佐久間信久が戦死すると士気が落ち、旧幕府軍は富の森へ後退した。

　伏見方面では、土佐藩兵が新政府軍に加わった。

　旧幕府軍は敗走した。

　朝廷は仁和寺宮を征討大将軍に任命し、錦の御旗を与えた。旧幕府軍は錦の御旗の行進を見て動揺した。

The Shogunate army was conducted by army magistrate Takenaka. About 600 of united armies composed of Satsuma and Choshu made the position surrounded Fushimi magistrate's office. Although Aizu clan soldiers and Shinsengumi in Fushimi office attacked the surrounding army by using big guns and short guns. A shell of the big gun of Satsuma hit the ammunition warehouse of Fushimi magistrate office.

Fushimi magistrate office went up in flames. New government armies shot guns with setting fire to neighboring citizen's houses. According to the withdraw of the old Shogunate army, Fushimi magistrate office was occupied by the new government army.

In Omi district, the Hikone clan, a big clan in hereditary vassalage to Tokugawa, added to the new government army. On January 4, the old Shogunate increased its power temporarily. However, the death of Nobuhisa Sakuma, army president, decreased fighting spirit of the Shogunate army.

Therefore, the old Shogunate army backed to Tominomori. In Fushimi, soldiers of the Toba clan added to the new government army. The old Shogunate army escaped anywhere. The Court appointed Ninnajinomiya the subjugation president. Kichinosuke gave Ninnajinomiya the Imperial standard. To see the standard marching on, soldiers of the old Shogunate unsettled.

1月5日、伏見地区の旧幕府軍は淀千両松でさらに敗退した。また、鳥羽地区の旧幕府軍も富の森から敗走した。淀城は老中稲葉正邦の居城なので、旧幕府軍は入ろうとしたが正邦不在のため、入城できなかった。やむなく、男山、橋本方面に撤退した。

　この日の戦闘で新撰組の3分の1が戦死した。

　1月6日、旧幕府軍は東に男山、西に淀川、南に楠葉台場を背にして布陣し、地形的に有利であった。

　ところが、淀川沿いにいた津藩が朝廷の命により裏切り、旧幕府軍に砲撃を加えた。

　旧幕府軍は戦意を失って総崩れとなり、淀川を下って大阪城に逃げた。

　慶喜は風邪をひいていたため、鎧を着ることはなかった。

　戦場には一度も姿をみせなかった。

　「この城にはまだ6000の兵がいる。籠城して戦えば負けることはない」

　慶喜は檄をとばした。

　しかし、彼は老中2人、元京都守護職松平容保と4人で城を抜け出し、船で江戸に帰ってしまった。

On January 5, the old Shogunate army in Fushimi district was defeated at Yodo-Senryomatsu. Also, the old Shogunate army in Toba district escaped from Tominomori. As Yodo Castle was the residence of Masakuni Inaba, principal retainers of old Shogunate, soldiers of the Shogunate tried to enter it. But they could not enter the castle by the absence of the lord. Unavoidably they escaped to Otokoyama and Hashimoto. About 33 % of Shinsengumi were killed in the battle on that day.

On January 6, the position of the old Shogunate army was taken up surrounded with Otokoyama east, Yodo river west, and Kusubahill south. It was considered to be advantageous geographically. But, the Tsu clan staying along Yodo river betrayed by order of the Court. Soldiers of the Tsu clan fired shells of big guns to the old Shogunate. The old Shogunate army collapsed completely losing their fighting spirits. They escaped to Osaka Castle going down Yodo river. Yoshinobu never wore the armor owing to a cold. He had never seen in battle field.

"We have 6,000 of soldiers in this castle yet. We shall never be defeated if we fight keeping ourselves in the castle." Yoshinobu encouraged soldiers. But he escaped from the castle with Katamori Matsudaira, former Kyoto protector, and two principal retainers. And he returned to Edo by war ship in midnight.

第11章

　1月7日、朝廷は追討令を発表した。慶喜は朝敵となった。
　1月9日、新政府の長州軍が大阪城を接収した。
　1月の中旬までに尾張、桑名と西日本の藩が新政府に従った。外国は中立を宣言した。
　1月14日に吉之助は追討軍の参謀に任命された。
　1月15日に追討軍は京都から出発した。
　軍は2月28日に箱根を占領した。旧幕府においては、抗戦派と恭順派が混在していた。吉之助は、抗戦派武士は新政府に従わないと考えていた。
　慶喜は旧幕府の代表者に勝海舟を指名した。勝海舟は恭順派武士の一人であった。
　慶喜は江戸に帰った後、上野の寛永寺に謹慎していた。
　「これからどうするつもりですか」
　海舟は慶喜に尋ねた。慶喜は無表情で何も応えなかった。
　親藩と東北の藩は慶喜の弱腰に怒っていた。
　勝海舟は性格に柔軟性のある西郷吉之助と交渉することに決めた。海舟は手紙を書いて部下の山岡鉄舟に託した。山岡は箱根にいる吉之助に手紙を渡した。手紙の内容は以下のとおりであった。

Chapter 11

On January 7, the Court announced subjugation command. Yoshinobu became the enemy of the Court. On January 9, Choshu army of the new government took possession of Osaka Castle. By the middle of January, the clan of Owari, Kuwana, and west Japan obeyed the new government. Foreign countries announced their neutral position. On January 14, Kichinosuke was appointed the top officer of subjugation army. Next day, the subjugation army departed from Kyoto. The army occupied Hakone on February 28. In the old Shogunate, warlike group and obedient one were mixed. Kichinosuke was thinking that radical samurais would never follow the new government.

Yoshinobu designated Kaishu Katsu the representative of the old Shogunate. Kaishu was one of the obedient group. Yoshinobu confined himself in Kaneiji Temple in Ueno after the return to Edo. "What are you going to do?" Kaishu asked to Yoshinobu.

Yoshinobu never spoke anything with no expression. Samurais of the relative clan and north-east clan were in anger for the weakness of Yoshinobu. Kaishu Katsu decided to negotiate with Kichinosuke Saigo whose character was flexible. Kaishu gave Tesshu Yamaoka the letter that Kaishu had written. Yamaoka gave it to Kichinosuke who staying in Hakone. The contents were as follows.

「わが主、徳川慶喜公は恭順の意を示してきました。貴方が我々の立場を考えるなら、なぜ江戸城を攻撃するのですか。我々は12隻の戦艦を持っています。我々が九州、四国、中国、大阪、名古屋、横浜にこれらの戦艦を配置するなら、我々は貴方の軍と戦うことができます。あなた方が江戸の市街を獲得するのは難しい。貴方の軍を箱根の西に止めておきませんか」

「これはわが官軍に対する脅迫である」

吉之助は怒った。

松平容保と会津の兵は会津に移動していた。また、幕府、旗本は前将軍慶喜の安全のために寛永寺を包囲していた。

吉之助はすべての兵に箱根に滞在することを命じた。彼は桐野と村田を連れて江戸藩邸に行った。

旧幕府は江戸城に兵を集めることが出来なかった。

江戸城の取り扱いについて、勝と吉之助の会見が薩摩藩邸で行われた。吉之助は勝が江戸城の開放について申し入れた二つの事項に同意した。

　第一、旧幕府は無条件で明治天皇に城を譲渡しなければならない。

　第二、すべての武器は城に残すこと。

二人の交渉者は天領の返還については議論しなかった。これらの情報は瓦版で江戸市民に知らされた。

"Our lord Yoshinobu Tokugawa has been showing the mind of obedience. Why can you attack Edo Castle if you think of our situation? We have twelve warships. If we arrange these warships Khushu, Shikoku, Chugoku, Osaka, Nagoya and Yokohama, we are able to battle with your army. It would be too difficult for you to gain Edo city. Why don't you stay army in west of Hakone?"

"This is the threat to our national army." Kichinosuke was in anger. Katamori Matsudaira and soldiers of Aizu had moved to Aizu territory. Also, the Shogunate Hatamoto had been surrounding Kaneiji Temple for the safety of former Shogun Yoshinobu. Kichinosuke ordered all the soldiers to stay in Hakone. He went to the clan mansion in Edo with Kirino and Murata. The old Shogunate could not gather soldiers around Edo Castle.

The meeting about the deal on Edo Castle was held in the clan mansion of Satsuma. Kichinosuke agreed with two items that Katsu proposed about the surrender of Edo Castle.

The first:The old Shogunate must give the castle to the Emperor Meiji unconditionally.

The second:All the weapon should be left in the castle.

Two negotiators never discussed the return of the Shogunate territory.

This information was reported by Kawaraban to the Edo citizens.

江戸では旧幕府の武士からなる彰義隊が結成された。隊は1000人から4000人へと増えた。
　また、新政府は参謀を吉之助から大村益次郎に変えた。兵の数は1万人であった。
　大村は前線に薩摩兵を配置した。
「我が軍の兵を全部死なせるつもりですか」
　吉之助は大村に聞いた。
「そうです。薩摩兵は今日本で一番強い」
　大村は吉之助に答えた。薩摩藩は黒門の前に陣を構えた。桐野利秋と海江田信義が薩摩藩と肥前藩を指導した。吉之助は黒門にアームストロング砲を発射した。黒門だけでなく寛永寺の塀が焼け落ちた。
　多くの長州兵が寛永寺に侵入した。旧幕府兵は裏門に逃げた。不思議なことに、裏門の錠前はすでに外されていた。吉之助が寺の僧侶に錠前を開けるのを頼んでいたのである。旧幕府の大部分の旗本が根岸方面に逃げた。
　戦闘はわずか一日で終わった。
　上野戦争の結果として、新政府軍は江戸の西側を支配した。旧幕府軍は北の宇都宮と東の千葉を守らねばならなかった。
　吉之助は長州の山県有朋と薩摩の黒田清隆を庄内へ派遣した。

In Edo, the Shogitai composed of the old Shogunate samurais was established. The number of army increased from 1,000 to 4,000. Also, the new government changed the staff officer from Kichinosuke Saigo to Masujiro Omura. The number of soldiers were about 10,000. Omura arranged Satsuma soldiers as the front line.

"Are yo going to kill our Soldiers."

Kichinosuke asked Omura.

"Yes, Satsuma soldiers is strongest in Japan now."

Omura answered Kichinosuke. The satsuma clan took up the position in front of the black gate.

Toshiaki Kirino and Nobuyoshi Kaieda conducted the Satsuma clan and the Hizen clan. Kichinosuke shot an Armstrong big gun to the black gate. Not only the black gate but also the mural of Kaneiji Temple burnt down. Many Choshu soldiers invaded the Kaneiji Temple. The old Shogunate soldiers escaped to rear gate. Strangely, the gate had been already unlocked. Kichinosuke had ordered priest of the temple to open the black gate.

The most Hatamoto of the Shogunate escaped to Negishi direction. The battle ended in only one day. In the result of Ueno war, the new government army gained the west of Edo.

The old Shogunate army had to protect Utsunomiya of the north and Chiba of the east.

Kichinosuke sent Aritomo Yamagata of Choshu and Kiyotaka Kuroda of Satsuma to Shonai.

吉之助は明治天皇の指示により、新政府軍の征討軍参謀に復帰した。
　東北日本では、40の藩が新政府軍と戦うために同盟軍を作った。江戸は東京と名前を変えた。
　また、元号は新帝の即位以来、慶応から明治に変わった。明治天皇は新政府軍の到着以来、江戸城に住んでいた。
　吉之助は若い新帝に言った。
「貴方は文民の長でした。貴方は自分が同時に武官の長であることを自覚せねばなりません」
　吉之助は千葉の習志野で軍事演習を行った。明治天皇は軍服に洋剣を着けて現れた。
「あの男は誰か知っているか。なんと美しい訓練だ。これは」
　天皇は演習を賞賛した。
「彼は薩摩の篠原国幹です」
　東北日本では、31の藩が奥羽列藩同盟軍に加わった。
　新政府は会津藩の松平容保を死刑にする計画を持っていた。容保は京都守護職であったとき、多くの長州武士を殺した。
　一方、東北日本の多くの人々は容保に同情した。

Kichinosuke came back to the staff officer of the new government army designated by Emperor Meiji. In the north-east Japan, 40 clans made the alliance army to battle. An era had been changed from Keio to Meiji since the enthronement of the new Emperor. The new Emperor had been living in Edo Castle since the arrival of the new government army. Kichinosuke said to the young new Emperor.

"You have been the leader of civilians. You must realize that you yourself are the leader of the military officers at the same time." Kichinosuke performed the military training of Narashino of Chiba. Emperor Meiji appeared with military uniform and western sword on.

"Who is that man? Do you know. What beautiful training this is?" The Emperor praised the training.

"He is Kunimoto Shinohara of Satsuma."

In north east Japan, 31 of the clans added to the Ou alliance army of north-east. The new government had thought that Katamori Matsudaira of the Aizu clan should be received the death penalty. Katamori had killed many Choshu samurais when he was in the post of the Kyoto protection. On the other hand, many people of the north-east of Japan sympathized with Katamori.

旧幕府、新撰組、会津藩は宇都宮に進出して、待ち構えていた。

　新政府軍は緒戦で完敗し、列藩同盟軍に宇都宮城を奪われた。宇都宮城は北からの攻撃には強いが南からの攻撃には弱い。

　旧幕府軍は、わずか1000名の兵で城を攻め落とした。吉之助は板橋にわずかの兵を残し、薩摩、長州、土佐の精鋭を増援として宇都宮に派遣した。

　旧幕府軍は時間とともに劣勢となり、ついに城を奪還された。

　旧幕府軍は日光方面に逃走し、宇都宮戦争は終結した。

　新政府軍は北進し、矢板、黒磯を経て白河に迫った。白河は奥州街道を守る重要な拠点であった。江戸時代は譜代の有力大名が配置された。

　鳥羽、伏見の戦で敗れた松平容保は、会津に帰るとすぐ軍政の改革に着手していた。江戸城の無血開城で徳川政権が完全に崩壊すると、新政府はすぐ白河城を管理下に収めた。

　奥羽列藩同盟に加入していた仙台藩は新政府軍への反旗を表明し、会津藩と同盟し、白河城に進撃し、奪還した。

The old Shogunate army, Shinsengumi and Aizu clan, gathered in Utsunomiya and they were waiting for the new government army. The new government army was defeated in the first stage of the war. Utsunomiya Castle was ruled by the north-east alliance army. Utsunomiya Castle was strong against the attack of north direction. On the other hand, it was weak against the attack of the south direction. The old Shogunate army gained the castle by only 1,000 of soldiers. Kichinosuke sent strong soldiers of Satsuma, Choshu, and Tosa to Utsunomiya with some soldiers left in Itabashi.

The old Shogunate army became weak as time passed and they were taken over the castle.

The old Shogunate army escaped to Nikko. And Utsunomiya war ended.

The new government army went to the north direction. And they approached to Shirakawa by way of Yaita and Kuroiso. Shirakawa was the important location to protect Oshu roads.

There was arranged powerful daimyo for the location in Edo period. After the defeat of Toba-Fushimi war, Katamori Matsudaira came back to Aizu. He began to reform of the army system.

After the bloodlessly surrendered Edo Castle and the collapse of the Tokugawa government, the new government had Shirakawa Castle under control. As the Sendai clan belong to the Ou-reppan alliance of north-east, they declared to rise revolt against the new government. And they united the alliance with Aizu clan. They attacked Shirakawa Castle and they regained the castle.

吉之助は戦上手の薩摩の伊地知正治を指揮官に起用した。

　京都守護職であった会津への長州兵の敵意はすさまじいものであった。最高指揮官に長州兵を任命すれば、非戦闘員である農民や商人が被害を受けるおそれがあった。

　会津軍は火器を持たず槍と刀だけで戦ったので、5月1日の白河口の戦闘では682名の戦死者を出し、記録的な大敗となった。伊地知は稲荷山から大砲を撃つとともに、小銃隊で隙間なく攻めた。

　白河で勝利した新政府軍は、北上できる兵力がなかった。

　5月27日に土佐藩兵、6月7日に薩摩藩兵、22日に長州藩、23日に阿波藩が到着し、態勢が整った。総指揮官は土佐の板垣退助、総兵力2000名であった。

　対する奥羽列藩同盟は、二本松藩、会津藩、仙台藩で合計約2000名であった。

　7月29日に二本松藩は二本松城内に孤立し、家老以下420名が戦死または自刃した。少年兵40名は激戦の中で孤立し、戦死した。

　会津藩兵と仙台藩兵は自国へ逃亡することが出来たが、二本松藩兵は逃げる場所がなかった。二本松城には明治新政府軍が入った。

Kichinosuke appointed Masaharu Ijichi of Satsuma the staff officer. He is good at war strategy.

Choshu soldiers really hated Aizu soldiers because the Aizu clan had been in the post of Kyoto Protection. If Kichinosuke selected Choshu soldiers as the staff officer, they might have given damages to farmers and merchant who were noncombatants. Because the Aizu army fought with spears and swords but not guns, they lost 682 of soldiers in the battle of Shirakawaguchi on May first. It was devastating defeat. Ijichi fired shells of big gun from Inariyama hill. At the same time, soldiers with short shells charged without a break. The new government army gained the victory at Shirakawa. But they didn't have enough troop to charge to the enemy of the north district.

The Tosa clan on May 27, the Satsuma clan on June 7, the Choshu clan on June 22 and the Awa clan On June 23, arrived at Nihonmatsu respectively. The war system had been arranged. Taisuke Itagaki was appointed as the top staff officer. Total soldiers were about 2,000. The Ou reppan alliance had about 2,000 composed of the Nihonmatsu clan, the Aizu clan and the Sendai clan.

On July 29, the Nihonmatsu clan was confined then in Nihonmatsu Castle. Soldiers of 420 contained principal retainers were killed. And some soldiers killed oneself. Boy soldiers of 40 were isolated from other groups and died in the war. Aizu soldiers and Sendai soldiers were able to escape to their own hometown. Soldiers of the Nihonmatsu clan could not go to any other places. The new government entered Nihonmatsu Castle.

伊地知と板垣は会津領への攻撃を決定した。
　会津への入り口は母成峠であった。決定は東京にいる西郷に報告された。
　吉之助は越後と秋田の厳しい戦況を聞いていた。吉之助は若松城の占領が最も重要であると考えていた。
　新政府軍は薩摩、長州、土佐、大垣、大村、佐土原各藩の兵で構成されていた。
　総兵力は約2200であった。奥羽同盟軍は仙台藩の逃亡によりわずか800であった。
　８月21日、母成峠の戦争は午前９時に始まった。
　新政府軍は20門の大砲を使って、旧幕府軍を攻撃した。
　会津藩の兵は若松城へ逃げた。午後４時に新政府軍の勝利が確定した。
　会津藩主、松平容保は白虎隊と共に滝沢村に進出した。
　しかし、容保は戸之口原の敗戦を聞いて若松城に帰った。
　白虎隊の若者は若松城の白煙を見て自決した。彼らは白煙を城の崩壊と解釈した。
　１日で藩境が破られたことは会津藩にとって予期せぬ事であった。
　旧幕府軍の不利はだれにも分かった。

Ijichi and Itagaki decided to attack the territory of Aizu. The entrance to Aizu was Bonari hill. Their decision was reported to the vice-president, Saigo, of the new government army in Tokyo.

It was thought that the occupation of Wakamatsu Castle was the most important. The new government army was constituted of soldiers of Satsuma, Choshu, Tosa, Ogaki, Omura and Sadohara. The total number of soldiers was about 2,200. The Ou alliance army were only 800 due to the escape of the Sendai clan.

On August 21, the war of Bonari hill began at 9.00 a.m. In the early morning. The new government army attacked the old Shogunate army by using of 20 big guns. Soldiers of the Aizu clan escaped to Wakamatsu Castle. At 4.00 p.m. the new government army won the victory.

The lord of the Aizu clan, Katamori Matsudaira charged to Takizawa village with Byakkotai. However, to hear about the defeat of Tonokuchibara, Katamori came back to Wakamatsu Castle. Young men of Byakkotai killed oneself seeing the white smoke of Wakamatsu Castle. They knew that the white smoke was the collapse of the castle. It was unexpected incident for the Aizu clan to be defeated on border of the clan in a day. Everybody understood the disadvantage of the old Shogunate army.

吉之助は会津藩主松平容保に手紙を書いた。

　手紙は薩摩軍の軍監、桐野利秋によって容保に届けられた。内容は次のとおりであった。

「三春藩や仙台藩のように多くの藩がすでに降伏しました。あなたは越後軍の応援を待っているのかもしれません。しかし、彼らは少ない兵で戦ってきました。あなたは応援の兵を期待することはできません。あなたは籠城を準備するでしょう。我々は3000の兵と大砲20門を持っています。あなたは農民兵を持っていません。我々は婦人や少年を殺したくはありません」

　しかし、容保は新政府軍への降伏を拒否した。

　会津藩は薩摩の裏切りにより鳥羽伏見の戦で敗北した。

　会津藩の老人、婦人、子供は城の２階で暮らしていた。兵達は城の入り口から出撃して戦った。３階と４階は新政府軍の大砲の攻撃により、完全に破壊された。

　若い女性までも新政府軍と戦った。死者は井戸の中に投げ入れられた。こうした中でも、若松城は持ちこたえていた。

　越後では、河合継之助の重傷により、戦争の終結が迫っていた。

　吉之助は戦争の処理を考えねばならなかった。

　８月11日に、吉之助は新政府軍を率いて新潟に到着した。

Kichinosuke wrote the letter to the lord of the clan, Katamori Matsudaira. The letter was given to Katamori by Toshiaki Kirino, the inspector of Satsuma army. The contents were as follows.

"Many clam such as Miharu and Sendai has already surrendered. You may wait for the help of Echigo army. But they have been fighting with few soldiers. You can not expect reinforcement."

"You shall prepare to endure a siege. We have about 3,000 of soldiers and 20 gates of big gun. You have no farmer soldiers. We hate to kill women and boys."

However, Katamori rejected to submit to the new government. The Aizu clan suffered the defeat in the battle of Toba-Fusshimi due to the betrayal of Satsuma. The old men, women and children of Aizu clan had been living on second floor of the castle. Soldiers battled, coming out from the entrance of the castle. The third and fourth floors were broken by the attack of big guns of the new government. Even young ladies battled against the new government. The bodies were thrown in a well.

In Echigo, Tsugunosuke Kawai was heavily injured. So the war was drawing to an end. Kichinosuke had to think about postwar process. On August 11, Kichinosuke arrived at Niigata with the new government army.

奥羽同盟軍が組織された時、長岡藩は二つに分かれていた。藩主の信頼の厚い家老河合継之助は戦争への参加を決めた。洋式武器の準備により、長岡藩軍は新政府と互角に戦った。しかし、兵数が新政府軍より劣っていた。

次第に彼らの軍は押され始めた。

5月19日に継之助は長岡城を失った。しかし、彼は驚くべき戦略を実行した。7月25日に彼は再び長岡城を獲得した。

この急襲戦において継之助は右足に深い傷を受けた。

継之助の怪我により、長岡軍の戦意は衰えた。

米沢藩の兵は敵の妨害により継之助を助けることができなかった。7月29日、長岡城は新政府軍に奪われた。

継之助は会津に逃げた。彼は8月16日に会津領で破傷風によって死んだ。

吉之助が新潟に着いたとき、継之助はすでに会津領に逃げていた。新政府軍に就いた秋田藩は村上城を占領した。

吉之助の弟、吉二郎は長岡城の戦で死んでいた。

吉二郎の遺体は魚沼の丘に埋葬することが決まった。

吉之助が斉彬と江戸に赴任した後、吉二郎は西郷家の4人の妹の世話をした。

吉之助は黙々と吉二郎の墓を作った。

When the alliance army of Ou was organized, the policy of the Nagaoka clan was divided into two groups. Tsugunosuke Kawai, principle retainer, who was trusted by the clan decided to participate in the wars. In preparation for the western weapon, the Nagaoka clan army had a close match with the new government. However, the number of soldiers were inferior to the new government.

Gradually, their army was losing the battle. On May 19, Tsugunosuke was taken over Nagaoka Castle. But he employed extraordinary strategy. He regained Nagaoka Castle on July 5. By the surprise attack, Tsugunosuke heavily injured in the right leg. Due to the injury of Tsugunosuke, fighting spirit of the Nagaoka army weakened. The Yonezawa clan soldiers could not help Tsugunosuke due to the interference by the enemy. On July 29, Nagaoka Castle was taken over by the new government. Tsugunosuke escaped to Aizu. He died of tetanus in Aizu territory on August 16. When Kichinosuke arrived at Niigata, Tsugunosuke had already escaped to Aizu territory. The Aizu clan belonging to the new government had occupied Murakami Castle. It was decided that the corpse of Kichijiro was buried at Uonuma hill.

After Kichinosuke went to Edo with Nariakira, Kichijiro took care of four younger sister of Saigo family. Kichinosuke made the grave of Kichijiro silently.

米沢藩の非戦により、吉之助は会津若松城に行った。

　伊地知は戦上手だったけれども、なかなか若松城の天守閣に侵入できなかった。多くの兵と婦人の遺体が自然に放置された。あたりに奇妙な臭いが立ちこめた。それはこの世の地獄であった。

　「戦は2週間後には終わるでしょう」官軍の監査役、桐野利秋は吉之助に言った。

　藩主容保は吉之助に会おうとしなかった。吉之助は桐野に「適当な時期に降伏を勧告するように」と命じた。

　吉之助は庄内藩の鶴岡に向かった。庄内藩は新型の3種の銃を持っていた。彼らは東北の藩の中で最も強い軍隊と言われてきた。

　新政府軍の佐賀藩は軍の近代化を推進していた。新政府軍は佐賀の兵を庄内藩に送った。近代的な小銃と大砲による戦争が庄内の男仏川で始まった。

　戦闘は1カ月続いた。庄内藩は戦闘で優勢であった。

　しかし、東北戦争では米沢、仙台、会津が次々と敗れていた。庄内藩は新政府と戦う唯一の藩となった。

　ついに、庄内藩は戦争を停止することを決めた。

With no battle of the Yonezawa clan, Kichinosuke went to Aizu Wakamatsu Castle. Although Ijichi was good at a war, national army could not invade the main tower of Wakamatsu Castle. Corpses of many soldiers and women had been left naturally. There were strange smells all around there. It was a hell of this world.

"The war shall be end in two weeks." Toshiaki Kirino, the inspector of the national army, said to Kichinosuke. Katamori, the lord of the Aizu clan, would never meet to Kichinosuke.

"You should advice him to surrender in proper timing."

Kichinosuke came back to Tsuruoka of the Shonai clan. The Shonai clan had the new type of three guns. They has been called as the most strong army in the north-east clan of Japan. The Saga clan in the new government had been promoting modernization of the army. The new government sent soldiers of Saga to the Shonai clan. The modern war by modern short guns and big guns began around Obutsu river of Shonai. The hard battle continued for one month. The Shonai clan had advantage in the battle. However in the Tohoku war, Yonezawa, Sendai and Aizu were defeated one after another. The Shonai clan was the only army to battle against the new government.

At last, the Shonai clan decided to stop the war.

山県有朋と黒田清隆は庄内藩の取り扱いについて協議した。しかし、彼らは結論を出すことが出来なかった。

　9月26日に、黒田と藩主酒井忠篤は鶴岡で会った。酒井は降伏に同意した。黒田は農民の馬に武器と弾丸を乗せて新発田に送った。黒田は家老の石原倉右衛門だけが罰せられるべきだと吉之助に報告した。

　吉之助は酒井忠篤に手紙を書いた。内容は次のとおりである。

　「貴方の兵は非常に強かった。貴方が撤兵したことを私は感謝します。我々はとにかく内戦を続けてはなりません。

　我々の師である島津斉彬は外国との交流を教えました。薩摩には大砲作製の技術とガラス工場があります。どうか、薩摩に研修生を送ってください」

　酒井忠篤は庄内藩の処理を喜んだ。吉之助はまた若松城に出かけた。城明け渡しの儀式がこの時期行われていた。

　桐野は日本の伝統的な形で儀式を実行した。容保は処遇を桐野に感謝した。容保は会津藩の宝刀を桐野に下賜した。

　旧幕府海軍長官榎本武揚は北海道の函館に移動していた。

　明治元年（1868）10月、吉之助は鹿児島に帰った。彼は日当山の温泉に行って戊辰戦争の疲れを癒した。

Aritomo Yamagata and Kiyotaka Kuroda discussed the post war process of the Shonai clan.

However, they could not make a decision. On September 26, Kuroda and Tadaatsu Sakai, the lord of the clan, met in Tsuruoka. Mr. Sakai agreed with the surrender. Kuroda sent weapons and bullet to Shibata on the horses of farmers. Kuroda reported to Kichinosuke that only Kuraemon Ishihara, principal retainer, should be punished. Kichinosuke wrote the letter to Tadaatsu Sakai.

The contents were as follows. "Your soldiers were very strong. I thank you for the withdrawal of soldiers. We should not continue a domestic war any way. Our teacher Nariakira Shimazu taught us the communication with foreign countries. We have the technique of big gun production and a glass factory. Please send trainees to Satsuma."

Tadaatsu Sakai was pleased with the treatment for the Shonai clan. Kichinosuke went to Aizuwakamatsu Castle again. The ceremony of surrender was performing at that time. Kirino performed the ceremony in a traditional style of Japan. Katamori thanked Kirino for the treatment. Katamori presented the treasure swords of the Aizu clan to Kirino. Takeaki Enomoto, the president of the old Shogunate navy, moved to Hakodate of Hokkaido. On October 1868, Kichinosuke came back to Kagoshima.

He worked off his accumulated fatigue of Bosin war by soaking in a hot spring in Hinatayama.

五稜郭は西洋式であった。城は平坦で五角形であった。

　城は水を張った堀で囲まれていた。たぶん、もし城に多くの兵がいたら、将来にわたってその姿を維持したであろう。明治元年（1868）12月15日に旧幕府軍は北海道を占領した。彼らは函館に新政府を建設した。しかし、明治新政府は函館政権を承認しなかった。

　明治2年（1869）4月9日、新政府軍は乙部に上陸した。そして、3方向から函館を攻撃した。

　五稜郭からの旧幕府軍の攻撃は湾岸に達しなかった。

　一方、官軍の大砲の弾は五稜郭の櫓を直撃した。

　明治2年（1869）5月11日、官軍は五稜郭と函館市内を占領した。新撰組の隊長土方歳三は戦死した。

　吉之助が函館に到着したとき、戦争はすでに終わっていた。黒田清隆は髪を剃って坊主になった。そして、吉之助に頼んだ。

　「榎本武揚は私の大事な友人です。私は彼の命を救いたい。彼は日本の新しい海軍で働くことが出来ます」

　吉之助は榎本を許した。

　函館港では旧幕府の全ての戦艦が官軍によって破壊された。

Goryokaku Fortress was made in the western style. It was flat and Pentagon. The castle was surrounded by the moats which contained water. Perhaps, if the castle had many soldiers, it shall maintain its own figures in the future.

On December 15, 1868, the old Shogunate army occupied Hokkaido. They established the new government in Hakodate. However, the new Meiji government did not allow the Hakodate government to do so. On April 9, 1869, the new government army landed in Otobe. And they attacked Hakodate government from the three directions. The attack of the old Shogunate army from Goryokaku could not reach the gulf. On the other hand, the shells of the big guns of the national army hit the main tower of Goryokaku.

On May 11, 1869, the national army occupied Goryokaku and Hakodate city. Toshizo Hijikata, the captain of Shinsengumi, died in the war. When Kichinosuke arrived at Hakodate, the war had ended already. Kiyotaka Kuroda had his head shaved. And he begged Kichinosuke.

"Takaaki Enomoto is my important friend. I would like to help his life. He will be able to work for the new navy in japan." Kichinosuke fogave Enomoto. In Hakodate gulf, all the warship of the old Shogunate was destroyed by the national army.

第12章

　明治２年（1869）６月２日、吉之助は多くの幹部兵士と共に東京に到着した。明治天皇は吉之助に明治政府で働くことを要請した。しかし、彼は政府の職を辞退した。

　そして、鹿児島に帰った。雨期だったので、鹿児島の町は蒸し暑かった。多くの人が幕府がすでに消滅したことを理解していた。しかし、だれも将来の旧士族の生活について語らなかった。なぜなら、薩摩藩は多くの武士を抱えていたので、情勢は非常に不安定であった。

　東京では政治権力の争いが薩摩と長州の間で始まっていた。政府は桐野利秋を熊本鎮台の初代長官に任命した。

　大久保利通の主導により、262名の藩主が明治２年（1869）６月17日に藩籍を奉還した。

　明治3年（1870）７月、大久保と木戸は鹿児島を訪問した。この２人と吉之助は新政府の主要政策を議論した。

　「徳川幕府は多くの不平等条約を締結した」「我々は不平等条約の改正のためにアメリカとヨーロッパを訪問したい」。大久保は吉之助に言った。

　「多くの幹部が外国に滞在している間、貴方が政府を守ってほしい」。木戸は吉之助に言った。

　吉之助は不平等条約の改正に賛成した。しかし、彼は東京明治政府に行くことを拒絶した。

Chapter 12

On June 2, 1869, Kichinosuke arrived at Tokyo with many staff officers. Emperor Meiji ordered that Kichinosuke should work on the new government. However, he declined post of the new government. And he came back to Kagoshima. As it was a rainy season, Kagoshima city was very muggy. Most people understand that the Shogunate had already disappeared. However, nobody spoke about what living of old samurai was going to be like in the future. Since the Satsuma clan had many samurais, their situations were so unstable. In Tokyo, the struggled for power had begun between Satsuma and Choshu. The government appointed Toshiaki Kirino to be the first president of Kumamoto magistrate office. Under the leadership of Toshimichi Ookubo, 262 of the lord of the clans returned the land and people to the Emperor in June 17,1869. On July, 1870, Okubo and Kido visited Kagoshima.

Three men discussed the main policies of the new government.

"The Tokugawa Shogunate concluded many unequal treaties."

"We would like to visit America and Europe to redress treaty." Okubo said to Kichinosuke.

"We hope you will protect the government while many staff members are staying in foreign countries." Kido said to Kichinosuke. Kichinosuke agreed with the change of the unequal treaties. But he rejected to work at the new government office in Tokyo.

鹿児島常備隊が熊本鎮台の指揮下に置かれ、村田新八は砲兵隊長に任命された。新政府において、二つの派閥があった。山県有朋と西郷従道は封建制度は維持されるべきと考えていた。
　一方、木戸と大久保は近代的な国家を作りたかった。木戸孝允は西郷従道と山県有朋に外国での研修を命じた。
　従道はヨーロッパから帰るとすぐ兄吉之助を訪問した。
「ヨーロッパには様々な政治体制がありました」
「フランス国民は王政に代わる共和制を選びました」
「政府の役人は全世界の文化と技術を勉強すべきです」
　従道は外国における研修の必要を説明した。
　2回目の帰郷で、従道は留守政府の保護を頼んだ。
　明治4年（1871）1月、吉之助は大久保に明治政府で働くと答えた。1月4日、吉之助は激しく動き始めた。
　彼は山口、土佐、大阪を巡回した。
　東京に着くとすぐ、彼は内閣に対し、東京に近衛兵を置くことを提案した。
　この制度は新しい明治天皇を守ることだったので、大久保、木戸その他の役人が吉之助に賛成した。

Kagoshima regular army was arranged under Kumamoto Magistrate office. Shinpachi Murata was appointed to be the captain of an artillery. In the new government, there were two factions, Aritomo Yamagata and Tsugumichi Saigo had thought that the feudal system should be maintain. On the other hand, Kido and Okubo would like to make a modern nation. Takayoshi Kido ordered Tsugumichi Saigo and Aritomo Yamagata to study in foreign countries. As soon as Tsugumichi came back from Europe, he visited Kichinosuke, elder brother.

"There were various political systems in Europe." "The French nation selected republican instead of monarchy." "Government officers should study cultures and technology around the world."

Tsugumichi explained the necessity of the training in foreign countries. On the second home coming. Tsugumichi requested Kichinosuke to protect empty government. On January 4, 1871. Kichinosuke began to act hard. He went around Yamaguchi, Tosa, and Osaka. As soon as arrived at Tokyo, He proposed to make the Imperial guards system in Tokyo to the cabinet.

吉之助は新橋に古い民家を借りて住んだ。料理は得意だが、洗濯、風呂焚き、草取りなどは人にたのむことにした。

　初老の男性を雇ったが、本人が通うのは大変だと言って、住み込んでしまった。

　吉之助は岩倉使節団が帰国し、新政府の懸案事項が解決したら鹿児島に引退するつもりだった。妻の糸子とその子午次郎は武村の家に残して東京に赴任した。

「奄美におる先妻の子菊次郎を引き取りたいんじゃが」

　吉之助はおそるおそる切り出した。

「よかんど。あたいが菊草ちゃんも面倒みてあげる」

　さしあたり、10歳になった菊次郎を武村の家に引き取った。

　薩英戦争の混乱で郷中教育は崩壊していたので、藩校造士館に菊次郎を入学させた。

　近衛兵の制度を作ったので、村田新八、篠原国幹、辺見十郎太、池上四郎などを主に兵部省の役人に採用した。

　大久保利通の要望で村田新八は事務官として半年働いたが、若い明治天皇を武人として育てるため、吉之助は村田を宮内大丞に任命した。

Kichinosuke lived in Shinbashi old personal house. He was good at cooking. But he decided to employ a man who does house work such as cleaning heating the bath and weeding and so on.

He hired old man and let him live with him because he said commuting was hard for him.

Kichinosuke had already decided to return to Kagoshima after the hard work of the new government was resolved. He moved to Tokyo leaving his wife Itoko and his son Gojiro in Takemura village. "I would like to live with Kikujiro staying in Amami-Oshima island." Kichinosuke confessed timidly. "Don't mind I will take care of Miss Kikuso too."

Kikujiro had turned to ten years old of boy. The gochu education had collapsed in the confusion of Satsuma-England war. Kichinosuke had Kikujiro enter Zoshikan of the clan school.

Opening of the system of the Imperial Guards, Kichinosuke employed Shinpachi Murata, Kunimoto Shinohara, Jyurota Henmi as the Ministry officers.

At the request of Toshimichi Okubo, Murata had worked under Okubo. Six month later, Kichinosuke appointed Murata main staff of Imperial office to educate the young Emperor Meiji to be a warrior.

吉之助は明治4年から公務員制度、軍事制度、警察制度の改革に着手した。兵部省を廃止して陸軍省と海軍省を置いた。御親兵を廃止して近衛兵を置いた。明治6年に徴兵令を出し、自分は陸軍大将兼参議となった。

　府は東京、大阪、京都とし、72県を置いた。小学校を作り、義務制とした。各府県に国立銀行を作った。

　太陽暦を採用した。徴兵令を布告した。キリスト教の布教を許可した。地租改正条例を布告した。

　李氏朝鮮が明治新政府の国書を受け取らなかったことから日韓関係はこじれてしまった。明治5年にも使者を2回朝鮮に派遣した。

　板垣退助が武力を背景とした修好条約締結を主張したのに対し、西郷は武力を不可とし、礼服による訪問を主張した。西郷の派遣は閣議で決まったが、三条が天皇に上申した際、天皇は岩倉の帰国を待って、正式決定する判断をくだした。

　岩倉の帰国後、大久保、木戸の内治優先論が浮上した。

　西郷派遣に反対する木戸、大久保、大隈らが辞表を提出、岩倉も辞意を表明した。

In 1871, Kichinosuke began to reform the government officer system, the army system, and the police system. He abolished the ministry of military. And he established the department of war and the department of the navy. He abolished intimate soldiers and installed Imperial Guards.

He became army general in the army and Sangi, councilor and enacted Conscription Ordinance.

The modern prefecture system of Japan was established to three of Fu, Tokyo, Osaka and Kyoto and seventy two of Ken. The primary school were made. And this was compulsory education system. He made the national bank in each prefecture, adopted in solar calender, decreed conscription order, the propagation of Christianity, and regulation of land-tax reform.

In 1868, Korea under the Yi Dynasty refused the sovereign's message for Meiji government. So the relationship of Japan and Korea became complicated. In 1872, Japan sent the ambassador to Korea two times. Taisuke Itagaki contented that the conclusion of the treaty of Amity by military power. On the other hand, Kichinosuke contended that the visit with formal wear without any weapon. The cabinet meeting decided to wait for the return of Iwakura mission. After Iwakura mission returned, Okubo and Kido began to espouse the theory of priority of domestic security.

Kido, Okubo and Okuma were opposed the plan of the sending of Kichinosuke. Three men submitted resignation of Sangi. Also, Iwakura expressed the resignation of Sangi.

(Sangi=participant in government, councilor)

明治6年（1873）9月25日に参議の板垣、副島、後藤、江藤が辞任を申しいれた。10月23日、吉之助も辞表を提出し、続いて桐野利秋、篠原国幹、別府晋助、河野圭一郎、辺見十郎太が政府を辞任した。およそ600人の官僚、軍人、学者が次々と辞任した。長州の旧士族、前原一誠はすでに長州の萩に帰っていた。彼は新政府の状態について憂慮していた。そして、彼は三条実美に手紙を書いた。それはつぎのようなものであった。

　「あなたは西郷の復帰によって、薩摩と長州の均衡をはかるべきである。もしあなたが私の考えを実行しないなら、日本は多くの賢者を失うでしょう」

　板垣退助は戦争が上手であった。それゆえ、彼は戊辰戦争で多くの手柄を立てた。しかし、彼は国会が開設される必要があると考えていた。彼は東京に残った。彼は国会の開設を東京市民に訴えた。

　大久保利通はドイツのビスマルクの民族主義を模倣することを決めた。1870年にビスマルクはフランスを打ち破った。そして、1871年にはビスマルクはドイツの宰相になった。岩倉使節団は1872年にパリを訪問した。大久保はベルサイユ宮殿でビスマルクの演説を聞いた。彼の演説は自信に溢れていた。彼の外交政策はフランスの孤立化であった。彼は多くの国と同盟を結んだ。そしてフランスを取り囲んだ。

In September 25, 1873, Soejima, Goto, Eto of Sangi proposed the resignation. Toshiaki Kirino, Kunimoto Shinohara, Shinsuke Beppu, Keiichiro Kawano, Jyurota Henmi resigned from the government. Politicians, staff officers, service persons, scholars, of about 600 resigned from the government one after another. Issei Maebara former samurai of Choshu said. He had already come back to Hagi in Choshu. He was worried about the situation of new government. And he wrote to Sanetomi Sanjyo.

"You should strike a balance between Satsuma and Choshu by making Saigo's come back. If you don't carry out this, Japan would lose many wise men."

Taisuke Itagaki was good warrior. Therefore, he achieved so many feats in the Bosin war.

However, he had thought that the national Diet needs to be established. He stayed in Tokyo. He appealed to Tokyo citizens about the necessity of the Diet. Toshimichi Okubo had decided to imitate the nationalism of Bismarck had defeated France. And in 1871, he became the prime minister of Germany. Iwakura mission visited Paris in 1872. Okubo had listened to the speech of Bismarck in the Palace of Versailles. His speech was filled with confidence. His diplomatic policy was the isolation of France. He had the alliance with many countries. And he surrounded France.

日本は小さな島国である。地下資源も少ない。多くの軍人、政治家が朝鮮半島、台湾などを軍事力で奪い、植民地化する帝国主義思想を持った。大久保は日本に帰国してすぐ重要な障害物に驚愕した。

　文部大輔、江藤新平が起草していた民法草案である。男女平等、個人主義を認めるフランス型民法で、大久保としてはとうてい受け入れることはできなかった。

　江藤の考えに共鳴したのが西郷、板垣、村田らであった。大久保は江藤の失脚を出会いから考えていた。

　韓国問題は西郷、江藤らを征韓論者に仕立てるためのすり替えであった。将来の国作りの考えが不幸にも西郷と大久保では根本的に違っていた。

　村田は岩倉、大久保らが帰国した後もパリに残り、太政官に宮内大丞の辞表を出し、パリに残った。

　名目上の留学目的は音楽の勉強であるが、西郷の密命を受けてフランス、ドイツの軍政、行政を研究していたと考えられる。

　大量の軍人、官僚などが去った後、大久保は内務省を作り、自ら内務卿となった。

　内務官僚による旧士族の取り締まりと労働運動の抑圧が主要な目的であった。

Japan is a small islands country. Most soldiers and politicians had a thought of colonizing the Korean peninsula and Taiwan by military power, which was Imperialism. As soon as Okubo came back to Japan, he was surprised at a serious obstacle. It was the draft of civil law that Shinpei Eto the minister of Ministry of Education, had made. It was French style of civil low that insisted the equal right of men and women and individualism. Okubo could not accept it.

Kichinosuke Saigo, Taisuke Itagaki, and Shinpachi Murata agreed with this civil law. Since the first meeting, Okubo had thought that Eto should lost his position.

Sending Saigo to Korea as an ambassador was Okubo's tactics to make Saigo and Eto look like aggressors who tried to subdue to Korea. There were fundamental differences of opinions between Saigo and Okubo on the construction of new Japan. After Iwakura mission's return, Murata stayed in Paris by submitting resignation from his post to Ground Council of the State. The purpose of his study in Paris was music. Certainly, it was considered to be the study of military system and administration in France and Germany taken on the secret order of Kichinosuke.

After the resignation of many soldiers and officers, Okubo made the Ministry of Home Affairs ministry. And he appointed himself as the Minister of the Interior, which was mainly control of old samurai status and and oppression of labor movements.

第13章

　大久保は全権力すなわち司法、立法、行政を天皇が持つことを決定した。

　彼は明治天皇を神にするよう計画した。

　公家と高級官僚が天皇を取り囲んだ。公家が政治体制を支配した。

　新政府は欧米から高性能の武器を購入した。

　大久保は朝鮮と台湾の植民地化を山県有朋と西郷従道に命じた。日本兵が山県の命により朝鮮に駐留した。

　従道は吉之助に対して薩摩兵を自分に貸すように求めた。吉之助は500名の薩摩兵を集めた。これらの兵は長期間台湾に駐留した。

　大久保は製鉄業と重工業を興すように指示した。

　大久保は士族に一枚の小切手を与えた。これは現金に換えることが出来た。しかし、それは一回だけであった。

　「これは我々に対する手切れ金だ」

　旧士族は怒った。

　山口県では、前原一誠により萩の乱が引き起こされた。

　熊本では神風蓮の乱がおこった。

　福岡県の朝倉では、秋月の乱が起こった。

Chapter 13

Okubo decided that the Emperor Meiji had all the power of Jurisdiction, Legislation, and administration. He planned to make Emperor Meiji the god. The Court officers and high-ranking bureaucrats supported the Emperor Meiji. The bureaucrats ruled the political system. The new government purchased great high-performance of weapons from United State and Europe.

Okubo ordered Aritomo Yamagata and Tsugumichi Saigo to colonize Korea and Japanese soldiers were made to stay in Korea by the order of Yamagata.

Tsugumichi requested Kichinosuke send Satsuma soldiers to him. Kichinosuke gathered 500 of Satsuma soldiers. These soldiers had stayed in Taiwan for a long time.

Okubo ordered to develop the steel industry and the heavy industry. Okubo gave a check to a samurai. This was able to change it for money. However, that was only one time.

"This is consolation money for us." The old samurai class angered.

In Yamaguchi prefecture, Hagi-no-ran war broke out by Issei Maebara. Jinpuren-no-ran war broke out in Kumamoto. In Asakura of Fukuoka, Akizuki-no-ran war broke out.

旧薩摩藩には多くの武士がいた。なぜなら、真の侍以外の郷士がいたからである。彼らは武士の仕事のないとき農業に従事していた。明治維新により、彼らは給料を失った。

　吉之助は青少年の成長のために、私学校を設立した。そのために吉之助は、明治維新の褒美として明治天皇からいただいた金を使った。

　この知らせを聞いて、大久保は私学校に自分の金を寄付した。

　篠原国幹が校長に任命された。また、私学校付属の砲兵学校が設立された。村田新八が校長に任命された。

　生徒は薩摩、大隅、日向、人吉、熊本、庄内から集まってきた。

　吉之助は徳川幕府の末期に薩摩藩を指導した。

　明治新政府は吉之助の統率力を恐れていた。

　およそ、30人の若い警察官が薩摩領に侵入した。

　多くの警官は東北弁を話した。彼らは私学校生に発見され、逮捕された。スパイは激しい拷問をうけた。

　スパイの一人が吉之助の殺害計画を告白した。

　生徒達は、鹿児島市内の政府弾薬倉庫を襲撃した。

On the old Satsuma clan, there were many samurais. Because a gohshi existed except true samurais. They were engaged in agriculture when they had no work of samurai. They lost the salary by the Meiji restoration. Kichinosuke established the Shigakko for the growth of youth and boys.

Kichinosuke used the money given from Emperor Meiji as the award of the Meiji restoration.

Hearing this news, Okubo contributed his own money to the Shigakko.

Kunimoto Shinohara was appointed as the principal. Also, an artillery school was established attached to the Shigakko. Shinpachi Murata was appointed as the principal. Students gathered from Satsuma, Osumi, Hyuga, Hitoyoshi, Kumamoto and Shonai. Kichinosuke had instructed the Satsuma clan in the last days of the Tokugawa Shogunate. The new Meiji government were afraid of the leadership ability of Kichinosuke. About 30 of young police officers invaded Satsuma territory. All the police officers spoke Tohoku dialects. They were found by a student of the shigakko and were arrested by students. Spies were under gone hard torture. One of spies confessed the plan to kill Kichinosuke. Students attacked the ammunition warehouse of the government in Kagoshima city.

吉之助が参議を辞職して帰郷し、私学校を創設した後の旧薩摩藩には、大きく分けて４つのグループが出来ていた。

最大グループは桐野、辺見ら吉之助を担ぐ旧士族で、彼らは私学校生徒に大久保の悪口を吹き込んだ。

第二のグループは岩倉使節団として欧米を視察した大久保を中心とする人達、征韓論争後も政府に残った政治家、役人、軍人、警察官である。

第三は島津久光を中心とした封建制度にもどし、士族を守れと主張する人達である。

第四はどの派にも属さず無関心をきめこむ人達で、かなり多かった。

大久保が軍国主義、植民地主義、帝国主義、天皇への権力集中、重工業重視を国策の柱としたのに対し、吉之助はフランス型の個人主義、共和制を計画していたと考えられる。

文久２年（1862）以降、村田新八は常に吉之助の密命を受けて活動している。彼は吉之助を日本最初の宰相にするのが自分の夢であると多くの人に語っている。

岩倉使節団全員が日本に帰国後、宮内庁に辞表を出して村田がパリに残ったのは、フランスの共和制を研究していたからに違いない。

After the resignation of Sangi, Kichinosuke came back to Kagoshima. He established the Shigakko. In those days, there were four main group in Kagoshima. The biggest group were old samurai class such as Kirino and Henmi. They had been supporting Kichinosuke Saigo. Kirino and Henmi informed the Shigakko students Okubo's bad reputation. The second group were persons who experienced United States and Europe as Iwakura mission. And they were person who had remained in Meiji government even after political change of 1873.

The third group were persons who supporting feudal system and samurai class such as Hisamitsu Shimazu. The fourth was a group of person who seemed to be indifferent to politics.

Toshimichi Okubo insisted on militarism,colonialism, imperialism, power concentration to the Emperor and promotion of heavy industries.

On the other hand, Kichinosuke Saigo had planned individualism of France style and republican system. Since 1862, Shinpachi Murata had acted taking orders from Kichinosuke.

Murata always said to everybody. "Our dream is to make teacher Saigo the first prime minister of Japan."

After the return of Iwakura mission, Murata submitted the resignation of educational staff of the Emperor Meiji and remained in Paris of France. That was because Murata must have studied the republican system of France.

明治9年（1876）、鹿児島の状況は緊張の極に達していた。なぜなら、多数の政府の密偵が鹿児島市内に侵入していたからである。吉之助の殺害計画が暴露されていた。土地税の増加が県庁の同意なしに決定されていた。

　大久保は反対したが、薩摩賊徒の討伐令が明治天皇の名で発表された。私学校の生徒が鹿児島市草牟田にある弾薬庫を攻撃した。この事件を聞いて、吉之助は根占村から鹿児島に帰った。緊急の会議が鶴丸城で開催された。

　「我々は西郷、桐野、篠原の3将を東京に派遣すべきである」。辺見が自分の考えを提案した。

　「政府の役人は途轍もない給料をもらっている。彼らは地方士族の困窮を分かっていない。彼らは我々に討伐されるべきである。彼らと議論する余地はない。我々は戦争を恐れてはならない」。池上四郎が叫んだ。

　永山弥一郎は武器の貧弱を理由に出兵に反対した。

　かつて郷中教育でしばしば行われていた討論において、村田新八は常に会議を主導してきた。しかし、彼はこの会議では、最初から最後まで沈黙を貫いた。

　島津久光は公武合体により、孝明天皇に大砲と銃を贈呈していた。

In 1876, the situation of Kagoshima had reached the maximum of the tension. Because many spies of the government invaded Kagoshima city. The plan to kill Kichinosuke was exposed. The increase of land tax had been decided without admission of the prefecture office. Although Okubo opposed the plan, the command was issued to subjugate Satsuma insurgents by the name of Emperor Meiji. Students of the Shigakko attacked the ammunition warehouse located in Somuta, Kagoshima city. As soon as Kichinosuke heard this incident, he came back from Nejime village to Kagoshima. The urgent meeting was held in Tsurumaru Castle.

"We should send the three leaders, Saigo, Kirino and Shinohara to Tokyo."

Henmi proposed his own idea. "Officers of the government have been receiving tremendous salary. They never understand the poverty and neediness of local samurais. They subjugate by us. There is no room for the discussion with them."

Shiro Ikegami cried. "We never afraid of the war."

Yaichiro Nagayama opposed sending soldiers due to their poor weapons.

In the discussion of the gochu education, Shinpachi Murata used to lead the meeting. However, he remained silent from the beginning to the end of the meeting. Hisamitsu Shimazu had presented big guns and short guns to Emperor Komei under the union of the Court and the Shogunate.

私学校において、村田は旧式の大砲と銃で射撃を教えていた。斉彬は集成館でポンド砲のような多くの大砲を作った。しかし、これらの武器は鹿児島に残されなかった。
　軍の進路は３つの経路が検討された。
　結果的に熊本路が選択された。薩摩軍にとって、政府軍と熊本城で戦わねばならないという困難な問題があった。
　政府軍は熊本城に食料と武器を搬入していると報告されていた。
「我々は10日で熊本城を占領することが出来る」
　桐野は自信に満ちていた。桐野は３年間熊本城で働いていたことがある。それ故、すべての参加者は桐野の言葉を信じた。
　明治10年（1877）１月、薩摩旧士族は戦争の準備を始めた。
　２月10日に吉之助は県庁と私学校に残されたすべての現金を集めた。その金は25万円と見積もられた。
　彼は２月11日に軍の編成と観兵式を実施した。
　篠原国幹、村田新八、永山弥一郎、桐野利秋、別府晋助が各隊の隊長に任命された。
　参謀の桐野が訓辞を述べた。
「郷士は城下士の命令に従わねばならない」

In the Shigakko, Murata taught the shooting in the old style of big guns and short guns. Nariakira made many big guns such as pond gun in Shuseikan. However, these weapons never left in Kagoshima. Three courses of the troop were investigated. As the result, Kumamoto course was selected. It was a difficult problem for Satsuma army to battle at Kumamoto Castle. It had reported that army was carrying foods and weapons into Kumamoto Castle.

"We shall be able to occupy Kumamoto Castle in 10 days." Kirino was full of confidence.

Kirino had worked at Kumamoto Castle before for 3 years. Therefore, all the participants believed Kirino's words. In January, 1877, Satsuma old samurais began to prepare for the war. On February 10, Kichinosuke gathered all the money that had been left in Prefecture office and the Shigakko. It was estimated at 250,000 yen. He organized the army and hold a military review on February 11.

Kunimoto Shinohara, Shinpachi Murata, Yaichiro Nagayama, Toshiaki Kirino and Shinsuke Beppu were appointed as the captain of each army. Kirino, main staff officer, gave instructions.

"Goshi must obey Jokashi."

薩摩藩の最後の家老桂久武が観兵式に来ていた。

彼はすでに還暦を過ぎていた。彼は兵の装備の貧弱ぶりに驚いた。銃は一発込めのエンフィールド銃であった。官軍は明治９年に集成館にあった連発式のスナイドル銃を大阪城に移していた。

桂は輸送隊長を引き受けてくれた。すでに国際赤十字規約が発効していたので、桂は荷車に赤十字の旗を立て、医者、看護婦、記録事務官も配備してくれた。

「桂さんにはこれまで何度助けてもらったことか」

吉之助は桂の手を握り、感謝した。

５つの大隊は２月13日から15日にかけて、出水ルート、人吉ルートに分かれて出発した。

11日から降り始めた雪は、15日には１尺以上積もっていた。吉之助は陸軍大将の軍服に身を包み、馬に乗って出征した。鶴丸城周辺には約１万人の市民が集まり、歓声を上げた。飛び跳ねる者、涙ぐむ婦人など喜びを表した。

加治木では3000人、人吉では5000人が薩摩軍を迎えた。

官軍は電信技術を装備しており、17日には第１陣が久留米に来ていた。

21日には、薩摩軍は谷干城が率いる熊本城を包囲した。

Hisatake Katsura, final principal retainer of the Satsuma clan, was participating in the ceremony. He was surprised at the poor equipment of army. A gun was Enfield type of single shoot.

National armies moved quick-firing Snider guns which were in Shuseikan factory in Kagoshima city in 1876 to Osaka Castle. Katsura undertook the captain of the transportation. Because, the rule of International Red Cross Society came into the effect, Katsura attached the flag of Red Cross on the wagon. He employed doctors, nurses and recording officers.

"You have helped me many times." Kichinosuke expressed his grateful for Katsura's help, shaking hands. Five armies departed from February 13 to 15 split into two groups, and taking Izumi and Hitoyoshi routs. From February 13 to 15, the snow was over 30 centimeters deep.

Kichinosuke wore military uniform of army general and he took the field riding a horse. About 10,000 of citizens gathered around Tsurumaru Castle. They gave big cheer. Some person leaped. Some women shed tears. About 3,000 in Kajiki and about of 5,000 in Hitoyoshi welcomed Satsuma armies. The national army had possessed telegram communication. The first army arrived at Kurume on February 17. On February 21, Satsuma armies surrounded Kumamoto Castle led by Tateki Tani.

２月19日、熊本城天守閣は原因不明の失火により炎上した。しかし、谷長官はこの事故に決して失望しなかった。

　城内の兵士は徴兵令で集められた農民であった。谷は戦争上手であった。彼は城の主要地点に兵を配置した。

　アームストロング大砲の弾は南熊本の薩摩軍を攻撃した。

　薩摩軍による激しい攻撃は３日間続いた。しかし、薩摩軍は城内に全く侵入できなかった。

　薩摩軍にとって不利な情報が吉之助にもたらされた。

　官軍は２月26日に田原坂に到着した。

　包囲軍の半分は、３月４日に田原坂の南の吉次峠に送られた。若い樹木がこの丘に生えていた。官軍が小銃を使うのは不利であった。しかし、もし彼らが丘を占領したら大砲の砲台を築くことが出来た。薩摩兵は丘の両側に穴を掘った。薩摩兵は穴の中に体を隠した。約600人の官軍兵が丘の頂上をめざした。

　突然、薩摩兵が刀で官軍兵を攻撃した。

　刀は腰の回転により、低い面から振られた。

　それは不思議な剣法であった。495人の東北の官軍兵がこの日の戦闘で戦死した。

　翌日の３月５日に官軍の本営は田原坂に移された。田原坂はだれもが小銃を使える低い坂である。

On February 19, Kumamoto Castle was burned in a fire of unknown origin. However, Major General Tani was never disappointed with this accident. Soldiers in castle were farmers who were made to gathered by the conscription ordinance. Tani was a good warrior. He arranged soldiers at the main point of castle. The shell of Armstrong big gun from the castle hit Satsuma army in south Kumamoto. The hard attack by the Satsuma army continued for three days. However, Satsuma army was unable to invade the castle.

The disadvantageous information for Satsuma army was given to Kichinosuke. The national army arrived at Tabaruzaka on February 26. The half surrounding army was sent to Kichiji Pass located in the south of Tabaruzaka. Young trees were growing at this hill. It was disadvantageous for the national army to use short guns. But, if they occupied the pass, they could install the base of big gun. Satsuma soldiers dug holes in both sides of the pass. Satsuma soldiers hid their own bodies in the holes. About 600 of national army soldiers headed for the top of the hill. Suddenly, Satsuma soldiers drew their swords against national army soldiers. Swords were swung from a lower level by swinging the hips. It was a strange sword technique. 495 of national soldiers from north-east Japan were killed in the combat. The next day, March 5, the base camp of national army was moved to Tabaruzaka. Tabaruzaka is the low hill where everybody could use a short gun.

3月の熊本地方は連日雨であった。吉之助は坪井川と井芹川の合流地点を閉め切った。熊本城の堀の水位は上昇し、石垣は水没するかに見えた。しかし、水位の上昇は石垣の上面の下70cmのところで、ぴたりと止まった。熊本城は水城へと変貌した。清正公は正確な水準測量をしていた。谷長官は西側の守りの兵を減らし、休養を命じた。

　官兵は昼間から酒盛りをした。

　田原坂では私学校生徒の驚異的な死闘により、一進一退の攻防が続いた。

　3月20日は10m先も見えぬ濃霧であった。薩摩軍は私学校兵を本営に引き揚げ、かわりに到着したばかりの熊本隊と都城隊を前線に配置した。

　突然100人ほどの官軍の抜刀隊が薩摩隊に乱入した。

　薩摩軍は戦の準備をしておらず、新兵は逃げ道がわからないので、大混乱となった。薩摩軍本陣に乱入した官兵は至近距離から小銃を乱射した。吉之助と幹部は逃げて、木山に本陣を移した。

　3月22日には薩摩軍の陣形は完全に崩れた。17日間の戦闘は終わった。

　両軍の死体が重なり、鳥も地上には降りなかった。

It had been raining in Kumamoto district in March every day. Kichinosuke dammed the point up where meet the two rivers flow together Tsuboi river and Iseri river. The water level of the moat of Kumamoto Castle began to rise. The stone walls seemed to sink out of sight. However, the rising of water stopped suddenly at 70 cm lower level than the top of the walls. Kumamoto Castle changed into to Water Castle. Kiyomasa Kato had conducted the accurate level survey.

Major General Tani decreased the number of soldiers in the west of the castle. He commanded these soldiers to have a break. Soldier had a drinking party during the daytime. In Tabaruzaka, the chance of wining battle was hanging thanks in the balance to the tremendous efforts of students from the Shigakko. On March 20, there was a dense fog which made it difficult to see something 10 meter ahead. The Satsuma army moved the Shigakko group to the main camp. Kichinosuke arranged Kumamoto group and Miyakonojyo group at the front line instead of students.

Suddenly, 100 of National soldiers withdrawn swords break into the Satsuma army's place. As nobody expected the combat that day, new soldiers could not find a route for an escape. They were in a panic. Satsuma soldiers got mass shot at point from national soldiers. Kichinosuke and other staff members escaped to Kiyama where they put the main camp. On March 22, the formation of the Satsuma armies broke perfectly. The battle that had continued for 17 days ended. Even birds would never go down on the ground owing to the overlapping corpses of the both armies.

4月20日、広い熊本平野で戦闘が展開された。

　薩摩軍の兵力8000人、一方官軍は3万人であった。午後には薩摩兵は緑川を泳いで逃げ始めた。官軍は泳いでいる薩摩軍の兵を撃った。川の水は兵の血で赤く染まった。

　戦闘はわずか一日で終わった。吉之助は兵達に5月30日に人吉に集まるよう伝えた。

　吉之助と将校は矢部村に逃げた。

　5月15日、桐野利秋は軍資金を稼ぐため、人吉から宮崎へ移動した。

　官軍は吉之助を殺害するため5人の刺客の女を送った。女達は黒い着物の中にピストルを持っていた。人吉の本陣はお寺であった。

　「もし俺がこの寺で殺されたら、俺は多くの人に笑われるだろう」。吉之助は笑いながら言った。

　吉之助はこの日の真夜中に人吉から宮崎に逃げた。

　5月31日、村田新八は1700人で3万人の官軍と戦った。

　村田は人吉城に大砲の砲台を構築した。彼は官軍の本営に大砲の弾を撃った。しかし、弾は官軍の本営に届かなかった。弾は商店街と寺に落ちた。

On April 20, the battle in the broad Kumamoto plain was fought. The national army had 30,000 soldiers. In the afternoon, Satsuma soldiers began to escape swimming in Midorikawa river.

National soldiers shot the swimming soldiers of the Satsuma army. The river water became red color with the blood of soldiers. The war ended in only one day. Kichinosuke said main soldiers to gather in Hitoyoshi on May 30. Kichinosuke said main soldiers escape to Yabemura village. On May15, Toshiaki Kirino departed from Hitoyoshi to gain the war funds. National army sent five women killers to kill Kichinosuke. Women had pistols in the black kimono. The main camp was at temple in Hitoyoshi.

"I shall be laughed by many people, if I was killed at this temple." Kichinosuke said with a laugh.

Kichinosuke escaped from Hitoyoshi to Miyazaki at the midnight that day. On May 31, Shinpachi Murata with 1,700 soldiers fought against 30,000 of national army soldiers. Murata installed artillery bases at Hitoyoshi Castle. He shot the shells of big gun to the camp of national army.

The shells could not reached the camp of national army. The shells fell down on shops and a temple.

この砲撃を見て、薩摩のために集まった約500人の人吉隊はどこかへ逃亡した。
　しかし、村田は大砲を撃ち続けた。官軍兵は火と煙により人吉城に近づけなかった。薩摩兵は小林に逃げた。
　その後、村田隊は小林と都城で戦った。彼らは激しい戦闘の後、敗れた。彼らは大隅半島を目指した。
　200の兵を率いる辺見十郎太は大口で官軍と戦った。彼らは緒戦で優勢であった。しかし、彼らは最終段階で敗れ去った。
　「もし、わが軍に私学校の生徒がおれば、最後は勝てたんだが」。十郎太は松の木の下で涙を拭いた。
　肝属川のすべての橋は官軍によって破壊されていた。村田隊はすべての兵が肝属川の岸で戦死すると考えられた。しかし、彼らは官軍の囲みを破った。村田と兵達は大崎村の松林に侵入した。彼らは志布志村へ走りに走った。
　彼らは夜明け前に志布志に着いた。
　短い休息の後、彼らは岩川、恒吉を通って福山海岸に着いた。村田は国分村をめざした。しかし、約4万の官軍が薩摩軍を待っていた。
　薩摩本軍は都城、野尻を通って宮崎に行った。
　江戸時代、宮崎市の南に旧佐土原藩があった。佐土原は薩摩の支藩であった。

Looking at the artillery fire, about 500 of Hitoyoshi group who gathered for Satsuma escaped somewhere. But, Murata continued to shell bombs. National soldiers never approached Hitoyoshi Castle owing to the fire and the smoke. Satsuma soldiers escaped for Kobayashi. After that, Murata group battled in Kobayashi and Miyakonojo. They suffered the defeat after the hard battle.

They headed for Osumi peninsula.

Jyurota Henmi with 200 soldiers fought against national army in Okuchi. They were at on advantage at the first stage. But, they suffered defeat at the last stage. "If we had had students of the Shigakko, we could have won the final victory." Jyurota wiped tears from his eyes under a pine tree. All the bridges of Kimotsuki river had been destroyed by the national army. Murata group considered that all soldiers must be killed on the side of Kimotsuki river. But they broke the siege of the national army. Murata and soldiers entered the pine forest in Osaki village. They ran and ran to Shibushi village. They arrived at Shibushi before daybreak. After a short break, they arrived at Fukuyama beach by way of Iwagawa and Tsuneyoshi.

Murata headed for Kokubu village. However, about 40,000 national soldiers had been waiting for Satsuma army. Satsuma main army went to Miyazaki by way of Miyakonojo and Nojiri.

In Edo period, there was the old Sadohara clan in the south of Miyazaki city. Sadohara was the branch clan of Satsuma.

吉之助と桐野は５月以来佐土原城にいた。桐野は宮崎で西郷札を発行した。西郷札はよく売れた。しかし、宮崎の人達は西郷軍に兵を出さなかった。薩摩軍病院で吉之助は長男菊次郎を見つけた。菊次郎は城東会戦で負傷していた。彼の右足は腐れつつあった。

　「私はお父さんと一緒に官軍と戦うつもりです」。菊次郎は父に言った。

　しかし、吉之助は菊次郎に言った。

　「私はお前が新しい日本のために生きることを望んでいる。もしお前がこの戦争で死ねば、愛加那はひどく悲しむにちがいない」。

　菊次郎は泣きながら聞いていた。

　吉之助は菊次郎を官軍病院に送った。官軍は宮崎に到着した。彼らは大砲で佐土原城を攻撃した。７月の宮崎は雨期であった。官軍は雨の日も大砲を撃った。西郷軍は宮崎から延岡へ移動した。薩摩軍の兵の数は村田隊と延岡師団の合流により3500となった。

　８月15日、官軍と薩摩軍は延岡の和田越えで激突した。

　５万人の官兵が山と谷に溢れた。

　「私が戦争の指揮を執る」。吉之助はすべての兵に宣言した。

Kichinosuke and Kirino had stayed in Sadohara Castle since May. Kirino issued Saigo-satsu-bill in Miyazaki city. The bill sold very well. However, peoples of Miyazaki never gave soldiers Saigo army. In Satsuma army hospital, Kichinosuke found Kikujiro, his elder child. Kikujiro was injured in the war of Kumamoto. His right leg was rotting away.

"I am going to fight against the national army." Kikujiro said his father. But, Kichinosuke said to Kikujiro. "I hope you live for the new Japan. If you die in this war, Aikana must be in great sorrow." Kikujiro was listening in tears. Kichinosuke sent Kikujiro to government forces hospital. The government forces arrived at Miyazaki city. They attacked Sadohara Castle with big guns. It was the rainy season in July in Miyazaki. The government forces fired the big gun even in rainy days. The Saigo army moved from Miyazaki to Nobeoka. The number of soldiers of Satsuma army became 3,500 adding Murata group and Nobeoka division.

On August 15, the government forces and the Satsuma army crashed at Wadagoe in Nobeoka. About 50,000 soldiers of the government forces filled in mountain and valley.

"I will take charge of directing the battle." Kichinosuke said to all his men.

辺見十郎太は長尾山に大砲の砲台を建設した。

　これが右翼の陣であった。奇兵隊は左翼として友内山に配置された。二つの山の真ん中に和田越えはあった。

　吉之助は和田越えの頂上で戦争を指揮した。官軍が最初に和田越えに突撃した。水田の水は深かった。官軍の兵士はぬかるみから自分の足を引き抜くことが出来なかった。

　桐野利秋はこれらの兵を攻撃した。多くの薩摩兵が桐野の真似をした。官軍は完全に敗北するかに見えた。しかし、薩摩兵はすでに弾を失っていた。官軍の応援兵が側面から弾を撃った。政府軍の海軍が援軍として和田越えに来た。ついに、全薩摩軍が敗北した。吉之助は旧友の児玉熊治宅に逃げた。

　8月18日早朝、吉之助は案内者により可愛岳に登った。

　彼らは谷の中に官軍の野営地を発見した。

　吉之助は600人の薩摩兵を4つの集団に分けた。

　全ての兵は自分の刀を抜いた。そして、彼らは大声を上げて坂を駆け下りた。官兵は薩摩軍と戦うことなしに延岡へと逃げた。彼らは多くの食料、武器、2万5000円の現金を残した。

　吉之助のフィラリア病が悪化しつつあった。

　村田は吉之助のための木製担架を作った。

　彼は吉之助を運ぶために4人の男を雇った。

Jyurota Henmi constructed the base of big gun in Nagaoyama. This was the position of the right field. Kiheitai was arranged in Tomouchiyama at the left field. There was Wadagoe in the center of two mountains. Kicinosuke directed the battle on the top of Wadagoe. The national army charged at Wadagoe at first. The water of rice field was very deep. Soldiers of the government forces could not pull their own legs up from mud. Toshiaki Kirino attacked these soldiers. Many Satsuma soldiers imitated Kirino. It was considered that national army would be suffered the defeat totally.

However, Satsuma soldiers already had lost bullets. Reinforcement of national army shot bullets from the side direction. The navy of government forces came to Wadagoe as the reinforcement.

At last, the entire Satsuma army was suffered the defeat. Kichinosuke escaped to the house of Kumaharu Kodama, his old friend. On the early morning of August 18, Kichinosuke climbed up Enodake mountain with a guide. They found the camp of the government forces in valley. Kichinosuke divided 600 Satsuma soldiers into four groups. All the soldiers drew their own sword.

And they ran down the slope with loud voice. National army soldiers escaped to Nobeoka without a battle against Satsuma army. They left many foods, weapons and the money of 25,000 yen.

But, Kichinosuke's filariasis was getting worse. Murata made a wooden stretcher for Kichinosuke. Murata employed four men who could carry Kichinosuke.

8月21日、薩摩軍は日向の三田井に着いた。およそ500の兵が吉之助に従った。農民と婦人が吉之助と兵の世話をした。

　「我々は西郷先生のおかげで猪肉やキノコを食べられる」。兵達は吉之助に感謝した。

　「西郷先生は悪天候の時、私達を助けてくれました」。幾人かの婦人が涙を浮かべて言った。

　軍は8月25日に鬼神野経由で銀鏡に到着した。全軍は古いお寺に野営した。吉之助と将校は寺の本堂に寝た。

　他の兵は大木の下で寝た。空気が冷たいので、兵達は5～7人の集団で火を囲んだ。兵の敢闘精神は衰えていなかった。しかし、鹿児島にいる老母を心配している兵も幾人かいた。兵達は短い睡眠を取った。

　8月28日、薩摩軍は小林に着いた。吉之助は旧友の庄屋を訪問した。吉之助は自分の考えを伝えた。

　「死ぬ準備は出来ています」。二人は別れの酒を飲んだ。

　薩摩軍は8月30日に横川、31日に蒲生に着いた。

　9月1日、彼らは鹿児島市の中央部を占領した。

　しかし、官軍は国分から鹿児島に帰った。

　薩摩軍は城山に移動した。吉之助は城山の頂上に本陣を構築した。

　官軍は3方向から城山を攻撃した。

On August 21, Saigo army arrived at Mitai in Hyuga. About 500 of soldiers followed Kichinosuke.

Farmers and women took care of Kichinosuke and soldiers. "We are able to eat wild boar meat and mushrooms owing to our teacher Saigo." Soldiers thanked to Kichinosuke.

"Our teacher Saigo helped us when the weather condition was bad." Some women said in tears. The army arrived at Shiromi by way of Kijino on August 25. All the army camped out at the old big temple. Kichinosuke and main staff members slept in the main building of the temple. Other soldiers slept under big trees. Because of cold air, soldiers surrounded a fire with groups of about 5 to 7. The fighting spirit of soldiers never be sunken. But, there some soldiers who had been worried about their old mothers in Kagoshima. Soldiers took a short sleep.

On August 28, the Satsuma army arrived at Kobayashi village. Kichinosuke visited the village headman, his old friend. Kichinosuke told his own idea.

"I have already prepared to die." Two men drank parting cups. The satsuma army arrived at Yokogawa on August 30 and Kamou on August 31. On September 1, they occupied the center of Kagoshima city. But, the government forces returned from Kokubu to Kagoshima. Saigo's army moved to Shiroyama. Kichinosuke set up the head quarters on the top of Shiroyama.

The national army attacked Shiroyama from three directions.

最後の本陣は政府軍によって占領された。岩崎谷へ逃げた吉之助は４日間洞窟の中に滞在した。

　吉之助の妻、西郷糸子が官軍の総督山県有朋を訪問した。彼女は山県に頼んだ。

　「あたいの夫吉之助にこん着物をば渡してくいやんせ」

　９月23日の夜、吉之助は洞窟の前で酒宴を開いた。

　すべての参加者が不思議なことに良い表情をしていた。

　村田はアコーディオンでセレナーデを演奏した。

　「なんと美しい音楽だ。これは」。吉之助は言った。

　９月24日早朝、官軍の総攻撃が始まった。

　桐野利秋は城山の頂上に立っていた。官軍の兵は鉄砲の撃ち方を止めた。

　桐野は自顕流の演武を披露し始めた。彼の姿は美しく、速く完璧であった。演武の後、彼は深いお辞儀をした。

　政府軍の兵達は小銃で弾を撃った。

　桐野の体は城山の頂上を転げ落ちた。薩摩軍の将校は洞窟の前に集まった。

　２発の弾が吉之助の腰と右足に当たった。

　「おいはここで死にたい」。吉之助は別府晋助に言った。

　別府は吉之助の側に来るとすぐ、吉之助の首を斬り落とした。

　およそ、190人の薩摩軍が政府軍に降伏した。

The last main camp was occupied by the government forces. Kichinosuke escaped to Iwasakidani. Kichinosue had stayed in the cave four days. Itoko saigo, Kichinosuke's wife, visited Aritomo Yamagata, the governor general of government forces. She requested Yamagata.

"Please, give this kimono to Kichinosuke, my husband."

On the evening of September 23, Kichinosuke held a drinking party in front of the cave. All participants looked fine strangely. Murata played serenade playing the accordion.

"How beautiful music this is." Kichinosuke said.

The general attack of government forces began in Shiroyama mountain in early morning. On September 24, Toshiaki Kirino was standing of the top of Shiroyama. Soldiers of National army stopped shooting of gun. Kirino began to demonstrate the sword technique of the Jigenryu. His figure was beautiful, fast and perfect. After his demonstration, he bowed deeply. Soldiers of government forces shot bullets with short guns. Kirino's body tumbled down on the top of shiroyama. Main staff members of Saigo's army gathered in front of the cave. Two bullets hit the waist and the right leg of Kichinosuke.

"I would like to die in this place." Kichinosuke said to Shinsuke Beppu.

As soon as Beppu came to the side of Kichinosuke, he cut down the neck of Kichinosuke. About 190 of the old samurais surrendered to government forces.

およそ、180人の薩摩武士が自決か戦死を選んだ。戦争の後、強い雨が城山を襲った。
　山県有朋は吉之助の顔を撫でながら言った。
「貴男はまさに日本の英雄でした」
　戦後の鹿児島の町には多くの乞食、売春婦、傷痍軍人が溢れていた。政府軍は町にビラを撒いた。
「西郷吉之助は市民の公金を奪った。我々は県庁にお金を一切見つけることができなかった。西郷のやったことは許すことは出来ない」
　しかし、だれもこのビラに関心を示さなかった。吉之助の人気はますます上がった。
　1878年に、大久保利通は石川県の旧士族によって暗殺された。1883年に、明治天皇は病床に岩倉具視を訪問した。岩倉は重病により起きあがることが出来なかった。
　彼は自分のベッドから天皇を拝んだ。
　1889年に大日本帝国憲法が公布された。国会は貴族院と衆議院のふたつの院で構成された。選挙権は15円以上の国税を納付した成人男子に与えられた。板垣の努力は報われた。同時に明治天皇は吉之助の官位を復活させた。明治政府は行政、医療、林業にドイツ方式を採用した。大日本帝国憲法は1945年に効力を失った。
　吉之助が西南戦争に勝っていたら、日本史は変わっていたに違いない。

終わり

About 180 of samurais of Satsuma army accepted suicide or death in battle. After the war, the heavy rain lashed down on Shiroyama. Aritomo Yamagata said stroking Kichinosuke's face.

"You were really hero of Japan."

There were many beggars, prostitutes, and deformed soldiers in the town of Kagoshima after the war. The government forces scattered a leaflet in the town. "Kichinosuke Saigo robbed of citizens official money." "We could not find any money in prefecture office." "What Saigo did was unforgivable."

However, no one interested in this leaflet. Kichinosuke was becoming popular more and more.

In 1878, Toshimichi Okubo died by the attack of old samurais of Ishikawa prefecture. In 1883, Emperor Meiji visited Tomomi Iwakura in bed. Iwakura was unable to stand up due to heavy sick. He worshiped the Emperor from own bed. In 1889, Japan Imperial constitution was proclaimed. The Diet was constituted by two House, the Aristocracy House and the Representatives House. The suffrage was given to the adult men who paid more than 15 yen of national tax. The efforts of Itagaki was recognized. At the same time, Emperor Meiji revived the official rank of Kichinosuke. The Meiji government adopted German style on military system, medical and forestry. Japan Imperial Constitution lost its effects at 1945.

Japanese history might have been changed if Kichinosuke had won the Seinan war.

The end

あとがき

　1876年12月に、吉之助は薩摩藩の元家老、桂久武に手紙を書いた。

　「私はもう一度大きな仕事をやりたい」。これは抽象的な言葉である。もし吉之助が最後の戦争で勝利を得たなら、彼はフランス型の国家を建設したに違いない。

　1884年に岩倉具視が病に伏した時、明治天皇は岩倉の病床を訪問した。岩倉は天皇を神として拝んだ。すでに天皇の神格化が始まっていた。

　大久保の基本政策は日本に大きな不幸をもたらした。日本は朝鮮半島と台湾を占領した。歴史の真実は真の帝国主義者が大久保、山県、大隈であることを証明した。

　多くの外国人が城山公園を訪問している。外国人は城山公園を西郷公園と呼ぶ。

　「西郷隆盛は憎むべき巨人であった。彼は朝鮮半島の征服を計画した」

　これには強く、異を唱えたい。吉之助は常に平和的な解決を望んだ。

　彼の重要な失敗は1873年の政変後の帰郷であった。彼は板垣と共に東京に残るべきであった。

Postscript

In December 1876, Kichinosuke wrote a letter to Hisatake Katsura, former principal retainer of the Satsuma clan. "I would like to carry out a great job one more time."

This is an abstract word. If Kichinosuke gained the victory in the last war, he must have established of French style nation.

When Tomomi Iwakura collapsed from a disease in 1883, Emperor Meiji visited Iwakura who was sick in bed. Iwakura worshiped the Emperor as the god. The emperor's divinity had already begun. The fundamental policy formulated by Okubo brought big misfortune on Japan. Japan occupied Korea peninsula and Taiwan. The truth of history proved that true imperialists were Okubo, Yamagata, and Okuma.

Many foreigners have been visiting Shiroyama park. They call Shiroyama park Saigo park.

"Takamori Saigo was a dreadful big man. He thought of the colonial occupation of Korea peninsula." I totally disagree with that. Kichinosuke always hoped for peaceful solutions.

His serious mistake was his home coming after the political revolution of 1873. He should have stayed in Tokyo with Itagaki.

■著者略歴 Author's profile

村本正博（むらもと・まさひろ）

昭和19年熊本県生まれ。鹿児島大学農学部林学科卒業。昭和42年、鹿児島県林務部に就職。本庁と農林事務所等に14年勤務の後、林業試験場に23年間勤務。植物病理の研究に専念し、マツの材線虫病、マツの漏脂胴枯病の研究で成果を上げた。平成元年10月にジョージア州にあった国立林業試験場で研修を受けた。平成5年に研究功績賞を受けた。主な論文はDistribution of Fusarium moniliforme var. subglutinans in Kagoshima Prefecture and its pathogenicity to pines.（日本林学会誌、1993）。資格は樹木医、測量士、実用英語検定2級。

Name : **Masahiro MURAMOTO**
the data of birth : March 11 1944
birthplace : Kumamoto Prefegture
last academic background : department of agriculture, Kagoshima Univercity
working career : He worked on Kagoshima prefecture office for 37 year. In this period, he engaged in the study of plant pathology for 23 year. In October 1989, he trained pitch canker disease of pines on national reserch center of Georgia state. In 1995, he received the best exploit prize of the study. Main article is follows. "Distribution of Fusarium moniliforme var. subglutinans in Kagoshima Prefecture and Its Pathogenicity to Pines."
Qualification : tree doctor, metrical surveyor, English certificate grade 2

大西郷の夢
The dream of Great Saigo

2018年4月20日　初版第1刷発行

著　者　　村本正博

発行者　　向原祥隆

発行所　　株式会社南方新社
　　　　　Nanpou Shinsha Kagoshima
　　　　　〒892-0873　鹿児島市下田町292-1
　　　　　電話　099-248-5455
　　　　　振替口座　02070-3-27929
　　　　　URL　http://www.nanpou.com/
　　　　　e-mail　info@nanpou.com

印刷・製本　株式会社イースト朝日
定価はカバーに表示しています　乱丁・落丁はお取り替えします
ISBN978-4-86124-379-0 C0023
© Masahiro MURAMOTO 2018, Printed in Japan